MW00640638

LEADERSHIP IS WORTHLESS . . .
BUT LEADING IS PRICELESS

LEADERSHIP IS WORTHLESS...
BUT LEADING IS PRICELESS

WHAT I LEARNED FROM 9/11, THE NFL, AND UKRAINE

THOM MAYER, MD

BK
Berrett–Koehler Publishers, Inc.

Copyright © 2024 by Thom Mayer, MD

All rights reserved. No part of this publication may be reproduced, distributed, or transmitted in any form or by any means, including photocopying, recording, or other electronic or mechanical methods, without the prior written permission of the publisher, except in the case of brief quotations embodied in critical reviews and certain other noncommercial uses permitted by copyright law. For permission requests, write to the publisher, addressed "Attention: Permissions Coordinator," at the address below.

Berrett-Koehler Publishers, Inc.
1333 Broadway, Suite 1000
Oakland, CA 94612-1921
Tel: (510) 817-2277
Fax: (510) 817-2278
www.bkconnection.com

ORDERING INFORMATION

Quantity sales. Special discounts are available on quantity purchases by corporations, associations, and others. For details, contact the "Special Sales Department" at the Berrett-Koehler address above.
Individual sales. Berrett-Koehler publications are available through most bookstores. They can also be ordered directly from Berrett-Koehler: Tel: (800) 929-2929; Fax: (802) 864-7626; www.bkconnection.com.
Orders for college textbook/course adoption use. Please contact Berrett-Koehler: Tel: (800) 929-2929; Fax: (802) 864-7626.

Distributed to the U.S. trade and internationally by Penguin Random House Publisher Services.

Berrett-Koehler and the BK logo are registered trademarks of Berrett-Koehler Publishers, Inc.

Printed in the United States of America

Berrett-Koehler books are printed on long-lasting acid-free paper. When it is available, we choose paper that has been manufactured by environmentally responsible processes. These may include using trees grown in sustainable forests, incorporating recycled paper, minimizing chlorine in bleaching, or recycling the energy produced at the paper mill.

Library of Congress Cataloging-in-Publication Data

Names: Mayer, Thom A., author.
Title: Leadership is worthless...but leading is priceless : what I learned from 9/11, the NFL, and Ukraine / Thom Mayer, MD.
Description: First edition. | Oakland, CA : Berrett-Koehler Publishers, Inc., [2024] | Includes bibliographical references and index.
Identifiers: LCCN 2023046636 (print) | LCCN 2023046637 (ebook) | ISBN 9781523006151 (hardcover) | ISBN 9781523006168 (pdf) | ISBN 9781523006175 (epub)
Subjects: LCSH: Leadership. | Crisis management.
Classification: LCC HD57.7 .M394 2024 (print) | LCC HD57.7 (ebook) | DDC 658.4/092—dc23/eng/20240108
LC record available at https://lccn.loc.gov/2023046636
LC ebook record available at https://lccn.loc.gov/2023046637

First Edition

31 30 29 28 27 26 25 24   10 9 8 7 6 5 4 3 2 1

Book producer: Westchester Publishing Services
Cover designer: Adam M. Johnson
Cover image: REUTERS/Larry Downing

For Maureen, always

CONTENTS

INTRODUCTION
GETTING STARTED

We have made life seem more complex than it really is. My experience leading people through some of the most challenging crises of our generation has taught me that things are in reality much simpler than most folks have made them out to be. This book is my fervent attempt to *keep things simple*, starting with this:

Leadership is worthless . . . but leading is priceless.

Such a contrarian statement requires an explanation.

When I recently checked on Amazon, I found that there are currently more than 60,000 books on the topic of leadership available for anyone to order and read. That's *a lot* of books! And when I asked the Google Bard AI chatbot service how many articles there are on the topic of leadership, I think I kind of blew its artificial brain just a little bit. The response was, "There are millions of articles on the topic of leadership. This is a vast and complex topic, and there is no one-size-fits-all answer to the question of what makes a good leader."

That might just be the smartest thing I've heard a machine say about the topic of leadership.

As you wade into this flood of books and articles, you'll find that their authors express the widest array of opinions, often contradictory, on this critical topic. They were written by a diverse and seemingly disparate group of people—from warriors who served their country courageously and admirably, to coaches, elite athletes, business leaders, and political figures. Many have been written by well-intentioned historians, researchers, and public speakers—too few of whom, unfortunately, have a deep history of having led teams in times of crisis, in different situations, across many boundaries, and on the world stage.

When I narrowed down my search on Amazon, I found that there are more than 550 books alone that include in the title or subtitle "Leadership Lessons from . . ." These include warriors (Navy Seals, Marines, Army Special Forces, British SAS, and others), coaches (Coach K, Greg Popovich, Pat Summitt, Pete Carroll, and Bobby Knight), explorers (at least five books on Shackleton alone), religious figures (every religion you could imagine), generals and admirals (Lee, Grant, Washington, Eisenhower, Patton, Marshall, Bradley, Nimitz, Puller, and Montgomery, among others), and even chefs (Jose Andres, Mario Batali). (And it can't be long until there is a *Leadership Lessons from . . . Ted Lasso*.)

I have read many of these fine books and have learned from all of them, each to varying degrees, yet substantially in the sum.

Given the plethora of books written on the topic of leadership, why am I adding yet another to the stack? Because none of these books focus on the central premise of the one you are holding in your hands right now, which is that *leadership is worthless, but leading is priceless*. Our fascination with leadership has obscured the fact that all of us, at every level of life, need not—indeed, should not—*aspire* to rise to a position of leadership. Because we are already leading all day, every day of our lives.

Understanding that insight is absolutely critical to your success as a leader. Move on from "*Someday* I *will be* a leader" to "*Today* I *am* a leader."

Among the many contrarian ideas expressed here, perhaps none is more contrarian—and ultimately helpful—than this:

Never use the term "future leader!"

Calling someone a "future leader" is a horrible, toxic, satanic, demonic, and disfiguring thing to label someone, despite what may be thought to be good intentions. Why? Aside from the somewhat condescending nature ("I'm a leader, but you are not . . . yet!"), it implies that your leading is only in the future, only when you have arrived at a higher level (which I have already attained, by the way), and can only occur "Someday" after a process of preparation, skill development, time, jockeying, positioning, cajoling, exhortation, and . . . luck. It implies "I have reached the godlike heights of being a leader . . . but, you, well, you have a ways to go." It ossifies us into focusing on "Someday" instead of focusing on the liberating word "Today!" So I argue that the term "future leader" should be banished from our vocabulary, no matter how well-intentioned we may have been taught that term is supposed to be. It focuses on the question, "How do I *become* a leader?" instead of the right question, which is "How do I lead *today?*"

Because the leader you are looking for is . . . you!

(To be sure, I am all for preparation and skill development, but those are to make you a *better leader* in an iterative fashion, not to make you worthy of the honorific "leader.")

This leads to the inexorable question, "Is this a leadership book? The answer is "This is decidedly *not* a leadership book!" But neither is it intended as an "anti-leadership book." It is a book calling for a redefinition of "leadership" and "leading" to transform us into a focus on the present and the multiple acts through which all of us lead, all day, every day, no matter what position in which we find ourselves.

I am often asked, "What do I have to do to build a resume to get a job like yours as the medical director of the NFL Players Association?" My answer is simple, if nonintuitive. On August 1, 2001, Korey Stringer, an elite offensive tackle for the Minnesota Vikings died of heatstroke during practice in the team's preseason training camp. I immediately received a phone call from my best friend, Gene Upshaw—a Hall of Fame left guard and the executive director of the NFLPA. Gene simply said, "Doc you are going to step up to the plate and become our first medical director." (Gene didn't *ask* these things and give you the opportunity to say no—he *told* you what you were going to do.)

Gene didn't select me because I had a great resume—he selected me because he trusted me. And he trusted me because his youngest son, Daniel, and my youngest son, Greg, were then and still are best friends, and our families had countless dinners (and more than a little Silver Oak cabernet) together over the years. We also coached T-ball (a game my father invented) together for our sons' team.

My point? Don't build resumes—build *relationships*.

Unlike other books, this one does not contain lists on everything from strategy to tactics to habits to *prescriptive* must dos. (Nor does it contain a list of *proscriptive* behaviors to avoid.) What it *does* do is to provoke—indeed *demand*—consideration of seemingly contradictory ideas, starting with the title on the front cover: *Leadership Is Worthless . . . But Leading Is Priceless*. I have extended the constant process of Socratic exploration of the dynamic tensions generated from questioning traditional wisdom in the chapters of this book:

- Why Leading Is Priceless
- Team Work . . . Or Teamwork
- Innovation at the Speed of . . . Trust
- Making Failure Your Fuel
- The C-Suite . . . and the We-Suite
- Don't Suck Up . . . Suck Down
- Slogans Are Worthless . . . But Actions Are Priceless
- The Healing Power of the Story
- Ask the More Beautiful Question
- Capture Data . . . But Treasure Wisdom
- Find Your Deep Joy

These ideas are estuaries, up which we must travel to reach our destination—a destination I hope you will find worth the journey.

While ambitious, my goal is to show how each of these concepts fits with all the others, like riprap on a pathway or breakwater, where stones are carefully selected and laid together to form a path forward or to protect us from storms. The chapters in this book are the stones that, when laid carefully together, become the riprap that will show you the path forward.

Each chapter includes stories, historical examples, and literary lessons, all of which have been selected to guide pragmatic and practical solutions, which can easily be put to work daily. This book is not a memoir, nor is it filled with simple personal reflections—although there are a few mentioned when they serve the purpose of illustrating leading through action. All of these are intended to help you embrace the idea and practice of *leading by living a life in the active voice.* (And I confess that the "Mayer Family Motto" has always been "Always do the more aggressive thing!" It has served us, our children, and our grandchildren well. Countless NFL players have told me that is precisely how they have lived their lives . . .)

Some of the insights you'll find in these pages are intuitive, while others are quite the opposite, yet none of them are complex. Indeed, all are simple, yet effective in my experience. My friend Mark Verstegen has changed the way elite athletes in every sport train to maximize their performance. His original company, Athletes' Performance, has grown into Exos, the most respected sports performance company in the world. Yet Mark's wisdom is reflected wisely and tersely:

Simple things done savagely well![1]

My hope is that this book does simple things savagely well— chapter by chapter, page by page, sentence by sentence.

My use of the ellipsis in the title of this book deserves a brief explanation. While derived from the Latin term meaning *omission*, I don't use ellipses to omit anything, except in an occasional quote to connect related meanings. Used here, it is meant to create a thoughtful pause or bridge between the dynamic tensions of "accepted wisdom" and the counter paradigm proposed. While a dash forces you forward, think of the ellipsis as a chance to pause, reflect, and reconsider. Reconsider what? Reconsider the conventional wisdom before an alternate wisdom is presented.

For example, when you read "leadership is worthless . . ." you might pause and reflect, thinking,

> Wait, leadership is worthless? Then why do so many people make such a big deal about leadership if it is worthless?

The chapters are intended to drive just that type of questioning of traditional wisdom. And for those whose literary tastes are prejudiced against our friend the ellipsis, consider the list of authors who used it successfully and repeatedly, including Shakespeare, T. S. Eliot, Mark Twain, James Joyce, Virginia Woolf, Langston Hughes, James Baldwin, and . . . Elmore Leonard. And for those wondering about that last name, he was not a great mystery writer (nor a great writer of Westerns before that), he was a great *writer*, and a master of dialogue.

Way back at the beginning of this century, the *New York Times* published an article written by Leonard detailing 10 rules for writers to consider as they worked their craft.[2] For the second rule, "Avoid prologues," he quoted an excerpt taken from John Steinbeck's book, *Sweet Thursday*: "I like a lot of talk in a book and I don't like to have nobody tell me what the guy that's talking looks like. I want to figure out what he looks like from the way he talks . . . figure out what the guy's thinking from what he says."

Consider ellipses as a conversational pause in our dialogue, where you can figure out what *you* are thinking from what has been said. As Twain notes in a penetrating essay on storytelling, "The pause is an exceedingly important feature in any kind of story, and a frequently recurring one, too."[3]

Two terms are consistently capitalized in this book for a specific purpose. "Deep Joy" is introduced in Chapter 1 and is discussed throughout the book. I capitalize it not out of any sense of self-importance, but because I believe it has a uniquely powerful meaning, representing, as it does, the force that drives us, our passion for life and leading, and our True North showing the way. Because of its central importance, I have chosen to capitalize it.

And I refer often to "The Boss," by which I mean the traditional (but outdated and unhelpful) concept of an individual who always seems to think he is the most important person in the room instead of realizing that leading means making everyone else feel that *they* are the most important person in the room. The Boss wields their rank and position as a symbol of their perceived power . . . and too often as a symbol of their self-worth, which is why I capitalize the term.

Regarding structure and how you might read this book, I suggest two approaches. One approach—the most common for any book—is to progress through each chapter sequentially. That's fine if that is how you prefer to read. But another approach is to first read this "Getting Started" introduction and then Chapter 1: Why Leading Is Priceless. After you've done that, you can jump to the chapters that most interest, and hopefully intrigue you.

Whatever your decision, it is the correct one because your curiosity best guides your learning—and leading. Each chapter begins with a quotation, which is intended to provoke you to think about the chapter's message before you dig in. I believe you must "read to lead," and I have personally selected these small pieces of wisdom to help you accomplish that goal.

Structurally, Chapters 1 and 2 frame the concepts that will guide your journey. Chapters 3 and 4 frame a structure to craft a path toward innovation and the critical role of failure in devising new ways of leading, because "The way we're working . . . isn't working." Leading in innovative ways across boundaries—particularly the authority boundary—and the importance of stories in leading are the subject of Chapters 5 through 8. How questions fuel innovative action and the importance of distinguishing between data, knowledge, and wisdom while leading are at the heart of Chapters 9 and 10. Finally, "Find Your Deep Joy" summarizes the viewpoints raised through the dynamic tensions within the preceding chapters. Each chapter ends with a succinct summary to guide action.

Because I am writing for a general audience—which is everyone, since my contention is that we are *all* leaders—I provide endnotes at the back of the book for any quotes or references contained in these pages. My intent is to provide you with additional material and sources of information should you be inclined to pursue them.

My challenge has not been what to say in this book, but rather what *not* to say. There are literally thousands of examples of the principles discussed in leading a life in crisis from my experience and from the experiences of countless others. My hope is that you will reflect on the experiences from your own life as you read, stimulated by the dynamic tensions in each chapter.

When I discussed my planned approach to this book with my great editor, Lesley Iura, the intent was to focus fiercely on terse, but engaging writing, so that anyone would be able to read it cover to cover during an airplane flight. I hope this brevity contributes to, not detracts from, considering ideas with value that have traction in your life. I wrote this book for one simple but compelling reason—to help people. I hope it helps you.

Good reading, good leading, and have fun!

Thom Mayer, MD
Wilson, Wyoming

1

WHY LEADING IS PRICELESS

> *The fundamental paradox of life is that the most
> important questions are simultaneously those asked
> least often.*
>
> —SOREN KIERKEGAARD[1]

The morning of September 11, 2001, was clear and bright in our nation's capital, Washington, DC, with a pleasant and persistent breeze
from the southwest. As the chairman of the emergency department
at Inova Fairfax Hospital, the regional trauma center for Northern
Virginia, and the designated trauma center for the president any time
he is south of the Potomac River, I started the day's rounds through
the ER, checking on the status of patients and the team of doctors,
nurses, and other professionals responsible for their care.

Shortly after 9:00 a.m., while rounding through the ER Communications Center, we saw a report on CNN that an aircraft, thought
at the time to be a small private plane, had struck the North Tower of
the World Trade Center in New York City. At 9:03 a.m., a second aircraft struck the South Tower, but this was clearly an airliner that had
been intentionally flown directly into the building. Then, at 9:22 a.m.,
we received a call from the Air Traffic Control Center at Washington

Dulles Airport on the red phone (which was supposedly restricted to calls from the Secret Service), with the most chilling message I had ever heard, "We have an aircraft unaccounted for."

Without hesitating, I turned to our communication nurse and said, "Activate the Disaster Plan. That aircraft is going to crash somewhere in the Washington area in the next few minutes."

At 9:37 a.m., American Airlines Flight 77 struck the southwest wall of the Pentagon at a speed in excess of 500 miles per hour. Although I did not know it at the time, two of my friends and neighbors were on board the aircraft.

I was asked to respond to the Pentagon that afternoon to assist in the ongoing rescue and recovery operation, rotating with other emergency physicians responsible for operational medical direction. Under police escort, I drove quickly to the Pentagon, following not only the police cruiser, but the black clouds boiling off the horizon to the east. The charred, gaping gash in the Pentagon, with smoke and flames still raging, gave me the same thought as everyone else who was there that day: "This *can't* be real." To a person, everyone who was at the Pentagon on September 11, 2001, said the same thing—it didn't seem real. It looked like the movie set for some airplane disaster film.

The other thought that came to me instantly was, "These are the Gates of Hell." And as I was about to learn, the Gates of Hell led to some interesting places.

The disaster incident commander handed me a bright, fluorescent-orange vest, labeled in bold black letters "COMMAND PHYSICIAN." It seemed to weigh considerably more than I thought it would—in both its physical and mental gravity. When it's your job to wear a bright-orange vest designating you "COMMAND PHYSICIAN," it is clear who's in charge. You cannot hide. Shakespeare's words came to mind: "Uneasy lies the head that wears a crown."

However, during the many hours I spent at the Pentagon—that terrible day, and the ones that followed—I learned an important lesson about leading. While there were several hundred people under my command, not only was I getting guidance from them, but they were teaching me much more than I taught them. I learned from structural engineers, paramedics, emergency medical technicians, firefighters, engineers, FBI Evidence Recovery Teams, and yes, even the Salvation Army volunteers who arrived on site.

All my life, people have told me—directly or indirectly, explicitly or tacitly, bluntly or obliquely—how important it is to show deference to those in charge, to respect authority, and to seek answers from above. The notion is that someone above us always has the answers. On September 11, I learned that the leader you are looking for . . . is *you*.

THE MASTER OF DISASTER

While many authors and speakers have researched, written, or lectured about leading in times of crisis, I have lived it—not just during 9/11, but many times before and after. Leading teams through some of the most visible and dramatic crises of our times is a brand I have been uniquely privileged to experience. The roster includes:

- Leading all health and safety efforts of the National Football League (NFL) Players Association (NFLPA—the NFL players' union) for more than 22 years.

- Leading as incident commander of the response to the first bioterrorism attack on US soil—the inhalational anthrax attack of the nation's capital in October 2001.

- Leading the NFL concussion crisis, changing the culture of head injury throughout all contact sports, as well as personally writing the entire NFL concussion protocol, despite significant resistance from the world's most powerful sports organization.

- Leading the NFLPA response to the COVID-19 crisis from 2020 to 2022, crafting negotiated solutions and protocols that resulted in the ability to successfully complete two of the NFL's most exciting and successful seasons, despite the challenges of a worldwide pandemic, lockdowns, vaccination hesitancy, and more.

- Leading the medical response to the DC sniper domestic terror attacks as medical director for Fairfax County Police Special Operations and Helicopter Unit.

- Leading the DNA analysis during the Duke lacrosse hoax, which resulted in dismissal of the case and the North Carolina attorney general declaring the players "innocent" in 2007.

- Leading a mobile emergency team deployment to Ukraine, sponsored by the NFLPA and Team Rubicon, caring for more than 350 internally displaced persons during the current war and training over 1,700 Ukrainian doctors, nurses, and paramedics.

- Leading the NFLPA's 2013 demand for all NFL teams to create Emergency Action Plans (EAPs), which directly resulted in the highly successful and internationally visible result when Buffalo Bills player Damar Hamlin collapsed on the playing field after going into cardiac arrest during a January 2023 game.

Maybe it's no surprise that my friends began to refer to me as "The Master of Disaster," a sobriquet that turned out to be prophetically accurate—time and time again. At the considerable risk of hubris, it is something about which I came to take a certain pride, because it is always an honor to lead a team of dedicated people in service of helping others.

I have been honored to give many speeches at national and international meetings and corporations over the years, including several times as the warm-up act for the great coach Lou Holtz. He makes it a habit to attend the speech just before his, both out of respect and to tie his speech to the one before—a very kind and generous habit.

After my speech on leading in times of crisis, during which I had mentioned many of my most challenging experiences, Coach Holtz began what proved to be a very moving speech. He turned his attention to me, sitting in the first row, and said, "Doctor, planes crashing into the

Pentagon, the first bioterrorism attack in history, players with head trauma . . . has it ever occurred to you that you might be bad luck?!"

Perhaps as the Master of Disaster I was bad luck, but it has been my privilege to serve others in those roles in my career. I was uniquely ready and able to step up and *lead*. Those experiences and many more taught me an invaluable lesson:

Leadership Is Worthless . . . But Leading Is Priceless

Why Is That True?

> Leadership is worthless . . . because it's a noun, the things you say—just words. But leading is priceless . . . because it's a verb, the things you do—actions, not just words.

However, leading is not only a verb, but a verb in the active voice. Everyone, at every level and in every job, organization, profession, and family, is actively leading through the things they do in these turbulent times of cataclysmic change, which is the fundamental nature of the world in which we live. They are leading themselves, families, friends, and the teams in which they work.

Don't wait to be summoned to a national or world stage to lead. You are already doing it. Don't focus on "future leaders"—lead today and every day. By focusing on "leadership," we have been focusing on the wrong question. To Kierkegaard's point, the most important question, but the one least often asked, is:

> How will *I* lead myself and my team today?

My experience has also taught me a corollary lesson, learned from Frances Hesselbein, former CEO of Girl Scouts of the USA who was one of the world's great experts and practitioners on the art and science of leading:

> *Leadership is a matter of how to* be, *not how to* do *it.*[2]

You must replace the wistful, passive word "*Someday . . .*" with the declarative, active word "*Today!*"

DON'T ASPIRE—EMBRACE THEN INSPIRE

So, you might ask, how can you move from *"Someday"* to *"Today*?"

First, **don't aspire** to be a leader, because you already are and you always have been. People have been treating leadership as a "someday" aspiration when it is a "today" reality we all face. This simple epiphany is essential to leading in the active voice.

Second, **embrace** the fact that you are leading and delight in it. Of course, there is both some good news and some bad news here (which is often the *same* news). The good news is that The Boss doesn't have what you want—it is already within and among you, personally, in teams, and in families. The bad news is that with the realization that we are leading, we can no longer lay the responsibility (or blame) on The Boss's desk. If we need to lead better (and we all do to different extents in different situations), then we have it within ourselves and our teams to do so.

Stop blaming The Boss—start leading your life.

Embracing your life as a leader is a commitment to live in the No Blame Zone, that special place where we know we have the answers *within and among us—not above us.* (And the No Blame Zone includes not blaming ourselves . . .)

Third, **inspire** every member of your team to lead as well. Leading and inspiring others to lead are inextricably linked—they cannot be separated. Your actions will inspire others to take actions to lead themselves and lead their teams, just as their actions inspire you in equal measure. Choose your actions and words carefully to reflect and inspire others to lead.

THINK, ACT, AND INNOVATE

I have three key goals for you to pursue as you practice the art of leading:

- Think
- Act
- Innovate

First, **think** about leading in a radically different way. The current paradigm of leadership is inadequate for the tremendous challenges we face today. It's essential to lead yourself and your team instead of waiting for your chance to lead.

Second, **act** on those thoughts within the week, because if you don't lead through actions within a week, I am sorry to say you probably won't act on them at all. Not because you are a bad person, but because that is simply human nature, as multiple studies have repeatedly shown.

Don't put your thoughts on a shelf; put them to work in your life—this week.

Like basketball or lacrosse teams, you are on a shot clock, but your leader shot clock is seven days long, week after week after week.

Third, **innovate** yourself and your team by changing the system— and yourself. Remember: The way we're working . . . isn't working. We live in times of crisis precisely because our challenges are both turbulent and disruptive. But as we will see in some detail, humans crave stability and being settled, even if they are at times unhappy with the ways that they live.

As we'll discuss later in this book, the speed of innovation occurs not at the speed of intelligence, audacity, genius, or even creativity. Innovation occurs at the speed of *trust*. It is all our responsibility to innovate, and not that of The Bosses in the C-Suite.

Leading is a constantly renewing process in which we think, act, and innovate to lead others and ourselves.

THINK, ACT, INNOVATE

One of my favorite people is Earl Thomas, the director of Environmental Services (EVS) at Inova Fairfax Medical Center, with whom I worked for many years. Earl is a kind, thoughtful, and generous person, whose immense integrity hides behind a quiet, calm demeanor. Earl has the difficult task of keeping a 1,000-bed tertiary care medical center clean and functional. In the past, EVS was referred to as "housekeeping" or, which is much worse, "janitorial services." If you looked strictly at their level of education, his team would be near the bottom rung of the ladder.

In conversations with Earl, I stressed that the medical center simply could not function without his team, since their work is not only literally the first thing people notice when they arrived (If the floor is dirty, how good could the medical care be?), but also that when patients are discharged from the hospital, the bed must be cleaned, which is the rate-limiting step or bottleneck for the entire process of getting another patient into the bed.

Earl told me:

> Doc, you've hit on the key issue. When we hire people for EVS, we make sure they know how critical they are to the institution. They aren't just cleaning floors or emptying the trash, they are the first step in people getting back to healthy lives. You can clean floors and empty trash anywhere, but if you work with us, you are part of a team changing lives. We thank them every day for being a part of the team. Somebody might say, it's still the same work, but we don't think so. I decided we have to think differently about the job to make it a better job.

Earl had taken the time to *think* about the job of EVS and how it fit into the institution, he *acted* on that thought quickly, and he *innovated* his approach to hiring and motivation to help the team understand its critical role in healthcare.

That's leading!

THERE IS NO LEADING EXCEPT IN TIMES OF CRISIS

Leading through multiple national crises led me to the conclusion that there is no *true* leading except in times of crisis. The crucible of crisis is the place where our actions define our leading.

Captain "Sully" Sullenberger shared a similar insight with me over dinner one evening in Wyoming, when he said, "You aren't truly a pilot until the engines go silent."[3]

"What are you until then?" I asked, wondering what those people flying airliners were actually doing when the engines were working the way they were supposed to.

"You are just a driver," was his immediate response. "A very experienced and highly trained driver, but still a driver."

The same is true of leading. You can only truly become a leader once the scatological stuff hits the metaphorical fan, otherwise you are just in charge—a caretaker, a manager. And being in charge but not leading is a horrible place to be.

The COVID-19 pandemic taught us many lessons, not the least of which is that every one of us lives in times of crisis and we will likely continue to do so for the rest of our lives, given the rapid pace of change in which we find ourselves. In the past, an appropriate metaphor for change was navigating the whitewater of Class V rapids in a kayak—exciting, exhilarating, enlightening, and . . . frankly, potentially dangerous.

However, once through the rapids, there were calm, placid stretches of the river where you could not only reflect on successfully navigating the rapids, but also enjoy the flat water and the scenery surrounding it at your own pace before the next set of rapids appeared. (And for those of you who have never kayaked, the paddle is not to propel you down the river—the river does that. It's to steer, stabilize, change direction, and ultimately, to keep you upright—all decent metaphors for leading . . .)

That was then and this is now. Today, we find ourselves in the perpetual whitewater of change. We shoot from change to change to change, creating the reality that the only constant in life is change. Most people don't mind *change;* they mind *being changed,* which is a far different process that we will learn more about in future chapters. Since leading only occurs in times of crisis, it will be a critical skill for all of us. We should expect crises, change, and innovation to be a constant companion—today, tomorrow, and beyond. World War II general George Marshall got it perfect when he said:

The choice is leading by action or losing by default.[4]

Too often we lose by default by failing to embrace leading and inspiring others to lead each day. Aristotle was correct when he explained:

We are what we repeatedly do.
Excellence, then, is not a virtue, but a habit.[5]

That's precisely why leading is a verb—we are what we repeatedly do.

Over the course of my 22 years in the NFL, I have worked with over 10,000 elite athletes. Not one of them has *ever* talked about leadership, demonstrating leadership, exhibiting leadership, or the principles of leadership. But all of them, in one way or another, have said some variation of the following:

Leading by example

Leading from the front

Leading teams

Leading by being

Leading every snap, all game, all season

They understand the verb "Leading" because it is something they *do, a part of who they are,* while "leadership" is an abstraction.

LEADING LIBERATES

Of the six presidents of the NFL Players Association with whom I have been privileged to work, Kevin Mawae is the only one so far to be elected to the Pro Football Hall of Fame in Canton, Ohio. I was honored when Kevin and his wife Tracy insisted that I attend the induction ceremony, where I heard him thank me personally, among others, from the stage during his acceptance speech.

One of the most importance insights I learned from Kevin came when he told me:

> Doc, you understand because you played the game. At first, leading seems like a burden—something extra you take on for the good of the team. But then you realize that leading liberates—it opens a completely new dimension to the game and you see things you wouldn't otherwise have noticed. By taking on the responsibility for others, you liberate yourself. That's how I got to Canton.
>
> Leading liberates.

For those who fail to understand it, leading can be horrifying, but in fact it is glorifying.

WHY LEADING MATTERS

I think we all know that leading matters, but all of us may not know exactly why that is the case. Here are some of the most important reasons why.

First, everyone at every level is a leader, in every action they take. You lead yourself and you lead your team.

Second, every leader is a performance athlete, just like my 2,500 NFL athletes, involved in an endless cycle of performance, rest, and recovery. As a leader, you invest in yourself and you invest in your team.

Third, the work begins within . . .

You might be wondering by now why I keep telling you that every person is a leader. Is it really true? Is everyone really a leader?

I have found in my many years of leading that this is a universal truth, though not as widely understood as it needs to be. Regardless of your position in life, and whether your title is mom, dad, sister, brother, clerk, entrepreneur, business owner, chef, restaurant server, bank president, bank teller, doctor, nurse, and on and on, you are a leader. You are leading your life, your business, your team, your family, your community, and more.

Leading not only has no regard for rank or social status, but it also has a healthy disrespect for titles, ranks, and other such false and arbitrary distinctions. Leading is life's universal leveler and democratizing force. Perhaps that is precisely why those in power or at the top have benefited from the false distinction that there are bosses and there are hired hands. What term could possibly be more demeaning than *hired hand*, as if The Boss wants your labor but not your mind?

HIRED HANDS

Julius Thomas is a former NFL tight end who played 70 games in seven years and had more than 2,500 receiving yards—excellent production for a tight end who was also a superb blocker. He played both varsity football and basketball at Portland State University—a rare two-sport athlete at a high level, who graduated with a degree in business administration. Julius won the NFL's highest honor for service, the Jacksonville Jaguars' Walter Payton NFL Man of the Year Award in 2014.

When I asked Julius what factors triggered his retirement, he said, "Doc, twice in the same year, two different coaches on separate occasions told me, 'Julius, I am not paying you to think, I'm paying you to run!' I decided I wasn't going to live that way and accelerated plans for the next phase of my life."[6]

Julius now has his master's degree in clinical psychology, is completing the last phases of his doctorate, and is the founder of Mastery Development. He is committed to using his mind, his soul, and his experiences to help others. He exemplifies the concept of servant leading, which requires constant thinking, reasoning, commitment, and compassion.

If The Boss wants you to *work*, but not to *think*, you may be in the wrong job. And if you are not willing to lose your job to do the job right . . . you may be in the wrong job.

To be clear, not every NFL coach believes what those two coaches told Julius.

For example, Coach Andy Reid of the two-time Super Bowl champion Kansas City Chiefs actively seeks the input of all his offensive coaches, as well as that of his All-Pro quarterback, Patrick Mahomes, before arriving at the game plan for every game, including the playoffs. This team input is essential in his system, as he believes it stimulates creativity and innovation.

THE STING OF THE WASP

On February 2, 2020, Super Bowl LIV in Miami's Hard Rock Stadium featured a close match-up between the National Football Conference Champion San Francisco 49ers and American Football Conference Champion Kansas City Chiefs.

With 7 minutes, 13 seconds left in the 4th quarter, the Chiefs trailed 20–10, and had just had a reception for a 1st down by blisteringly fast wide receiver Tyreek Hill overturned by a San Francisco challenge flag. This resulted in a 3rd down with 15 yards to go from their 35-yard line. Quarterback Patrick Mahomes, playing in his first Super Bowl, was not performing particularly well—so much so that announcer Joe Buck had just said that Patrick needed to play better and that the Chiefs needed some "Mahomes Magic" if they were going to win.

As referee Bill Vinovich reviewed the prior replay, Patrick spoke with Coach Reid and offensive coordinator Eric Bienemy. He asked, "Do we have time to run Wasp?" (By "time," he meant, did he have enough protection from the offensive line for the play, since Wasp takes a full 4 seconds of protection due to the deep route being run.)

In the huddle that followed, the play call was, "Gun, Trey Right 2–3 Jet Chip Wasp, Y funnel."

While that string of words might sound incomprehensible to most people, each word in a play call has a specific meaning to a professional football player. It's not unlike the way that as an emergency physician, my description of a "ventricular tachydysrhythmia with unstable hemodynamics" is completely clear to my team, but not to the average person. Here's an explanation of the call in detail:

Gun = Shotgun formation, with the QB lined up 5 yards deep

Trey Right = Tight end to the right and three wide receivers are lined up on the left side of the formation

2–3 Jet = Line protection call, with the offensive linemen sliding to the most outside threat for the left tackle and the right guard, right tackle, and running back are on the 2 defensive linemen and linebacker on the right side

Chip = 6 man protection package, with help to both offensive tackles to chip the edge and slow down the defensive ends—this is what will be needed to get the "time" Patrick referenced in his question

Wasp = Slot receiver Tyreek Hill runs a deep post-corner route, starting downfield, then cutting across the middle (post) before cutting sharply back to the outside (corner)

Y funnel = The Y receiver funnels toward the middle of the field, pulling the defensive back with him and clearing open space for the Wasp[7]

At the snap, Mahomes executed what was in effect a seven-step drop (most quarterbacks only take five). Defensive tackle DeForest Buckner of the 49ers had executed an outside stunt, looping around the left tackle, even with the chip on the defensive end, who had crashed down inside, and was bearing down on Patrick, forcing him to retreat, and just as he was hit 14 yards behind the line of scrimmage, he released the ball in a high arc. Patrick had gotten—barely—his 4 seconds of protection to make the throw, which came off his front foot, not his planted back foot as usual.

The 49ers were in a 3-deep zone coverage, known as "Cover 3," which in essence divides the deep coverage into three zones across the field. The cornerback, who had the outside third of the field, stayed with the wide receiver furthest toward the sideline, instead of covering Tyreek Hill, cutting across the middle from the slot. Before Tyreek made his final cut to the outside—turning the safety, who was now covering him, completely around—Patrick had released the ball, knowing precisely where Hill would be.

The ball traveled 57.1 yards in the air, an unbelievable distance yet right on the money. Hill caught it and was wrestled down at the 49ers 20-yard line for a 44-yard gain, turning the game around. The Chiefs went on to score on this and the next two possessions, winning the Super Bowl 31–20. Patrick had gotten the time to run "Wasp." The Chiefs has gotten their Mahomes Magic!

Why was this such a powerful approach?

First, Coach Reid's philosophy is a wise but nonintuitive one where, as important as *innovation* is, the key is the *trust* in his coaches and players to make suggestions at any time, without any fear of criticism or reprisal. That's diametrically opposed to *"I'm not paying you to think. I'm paying you to run."*

Andy Reid understands that every person on the team is a leader—lead yourself, lead your team!

Second, every team member, like all 2,500 of my NFL players, is involved in a never-ending cycle of *performance, rest, and recovery, performance, rest, and recovery.* Leading, while essential and universal, isn't always—or even often—easy. Leading is taxing, requiring energy, focus, and creativity as the challenges loom before us. Leading always involves failure, as we'll explore in Chapter 4. We must invest in ourselves and invest in our teams to replenish and reinvigorate our skills, preparing us for the next cycle, the next challenge, and the next crisis.

Leading by everyone at all levels, while exhilarating, is also exhausting. Take time to develop your resiliency/adaptive capacity. Invest in yourself, invest in your team . . . it's a solid foundation both in the NFL and in life. Performance, rest, and recovery is a cycle through which we all go. But too few of us take the time to invest in rest and recovery.

Third, *the work begins within.* In starting with ourselves, we attain the energy, motivation, will, and tenacity to change the system. To be sure, the system will need to be changed. Dr. Paul Batalden, a healthcare innovator, expressed it well (channeling thoughts of Arthur Jones of Procter & Gamble, who expressed a similar thought earlier):

> *Every system is perfectly designed to get precisely*
> *the results it gets.*[8]

If we are not completely delighted with the results we are obtaining (and no one ever is—at least not for long), then we must change the system, not just the people within the system. Too much of the literature on leadership focuses on exhorting the masses (often using posters and slogans) and getting the *hired hands* to work at their maximum potential. But to have the energy and tenacity to change the systems in which we live and work, we must first change ourselves.

Which leads to this corollary:

> The work begins within . . . but it turns toward teamwork.

We start by strengthening ourselves, but we turn quickly toward the importance of using that energy and adaptive capacity to build and maintain teams.

During the Russian invasion of Ukraine, our Mobile Emergency Team, Med Team A, comprised Dr. Dave Young and me as emergency physicians, Liane and Summer, our badass nurses, Chris, our flight-trained PA (physician assistant), Steve, our firefighter, Breaux, our team lead and firefighter, as well as Earl, who led logistics for the entire team. These individuals came from all over the country to the war zone of Ukraine, but we were not individuals— we were a driven, passionate, cohesive team, leading our parts of the whole.

In the next chapter, we'll discuss the importance of leading teams, but we start with ourselves, embracing the fact that we lead all day, every day, in every action. Leading matters because everyone at every level will spend every day of their lives in the crucible of crisis and change. In leading yourself, you lay the foundation for leading your teams. In changing the lives of others, you change your own life. In leading toward possibility, you lead away from deniability and those who constantly crow, "That'll never work!"

But as Wayne Gretzky, one of the greatest leaders in the National Hockey League once said:

You miss 100 percent of the shots you don't take.[9]

Take your shot!

(To emphasize the role of teamwork, remember that Gretzky is the leading goal scorer in NHL history at 894 goals . . . but he also had 1,963 assists. And Matt Danowski, my son's teammate at Duke, was the leading goal scorer in Division I lacrosse history when he graduated at 170 goals . . . but he also had 183 assists. Great leaders may attain glory, but they are even more generous to their teammates.)

DISCOVERING DEEP JOY AND LEADING

My beautiful and brilliant wife, Maureen, and I have three wonderful sons, now grown men. When they were younger, whenever I was in town, I drove them to school in the morning. And when I dropped them off, I always said precisely the same thing to them, which was:

One more step in the journey of discovering where your
Deep Joy intersects the world's deep needs.

I swear I said that to them. They preferred to take the bus! The point is simple, but important. The world's deep needs are infinite and often impenetrable. You must start with—and stay constant to—your Deep Joy! Everything else is a distraction.

Burnout occurs when we allow the job stressors to disconnect us from our Deep Joy. Reconnecting to our Deep Joy—our True North, our *raison d'être*—is the core of curing burnout, and the core of leading in times of crisis.

You may also refer to Deep Joy as your passion, and this is a perfectly reasonable formulation as well. In following our Deep Joy or passion, we are constantly reminded (preferably every day in every interaction) of the extent to which those actions are true to the Deep Joy. Sun Tzu understood this as he clearly demonstrated, in his wonderfully terse way in *The Art of War*:

Every battle is won before it is fought.[10]

The battle is won by those who know their Deep Joy and stay true to it. To be blunt, this isn't always easy—in fact, it is never easy at first to say, "While this looks like a great short-term opportunity, I must say 'No' because it takes me away from my Deep Joy." That's hard, that's tough. The only thing harder and tougher is to cave in and do the expedient thing . . . and then navigate your way back eventually.

MAKING MONEY OR UNLEASHING DREAMS?

Last year I had the pleasure of speaking to an elite group of wealth management leaders who work with sophisticated clients. Their managing partner asked me to discuss leading in times of crisis amidst the churning financial markets. After telling them the story of our boys and Deep Joy, I asked the group to do an exercise by reflecting upon and then discussing their own Deep Joy.

At first, the responses were largely along the lines of "increasing wealth for my clients" and "making the most of the turmoil in the financial markets." But as we drilled down to why they had chosen this work and what they loved most about it the answers changed from strictly financial wealth to a different type of wealth.

Gradually but inexorably, as I asked them to get deeper to the core of what motivated them, one of them said, "My Deep Joy is to unleash dreams for people, protecting their hard-earned wealth and giving them access to dreams they might otherwise never have been able to imagine." In the stunned silence, there were many, many smiles . . . and more than a few tears. Often, you must drill down to get to the bedrock of people's hidden Deep Joy—but it is always there.

Many people protect themselves with the patina of superficiality, but their Deep Joy inevitably derives from a deeper meaning than just numbers.

REVERSE THE JUMP

As a physician, part of my Deep Joy has been caring for patients—people from all walks of life—who have taught and given me much more than I could ever give them in return. In my work with health-care systems, I show them a photo of a young female physician jumping for joy and ask them a simple question:

> While the photo is of a physician, it could just as easily be anyone doing any job anywhere. Regardless of what kind of work you do, I have a question to ask: Is that *you*?

Now, let me ask a follow-up question: "Is that you? Going *in* to work . . . or going *home*?" Because it is my contention that all of us, no matter where we work or what we do, deserves to feel that way going *in* to work, not just *going home*. To do that, we need to *reverse the jump*, and the first step in doing that is to reconnect to our Deep Joy, which is critical to leading authentically and with intentionality. Leading requires unleashing that jump for joy in all of us.

Here are two ways you can reconnect to your Deep Joy:

First, get a photo of yourself in your formative years. It might be from grade school, junior high, high school, college, your first job, your best job, or the day you were married. Now explain to that young person in the picture what your Deep Joy was. Tell her if and how you have stayed true to that Deep Joy. If not, why not? And if not, how will you navigate your way back to it? (Hint: It starts by leading in every action of every day . . .)

Second, some people prefer to use the magical tool of the written word, using simple declarative sentences. If you're one of those folks, write a letter . . . to yourself . . . from yourself—the person you have become. Answer the same questions as above. Don't be surprised if either path becomes a bit emotional—these are matters of the heart, not just the head. And don't despair. I guarantee there are ways to re-connect with your Deep Joy, which we'll share together throughout this book. Your journey back to it can be transformational.

And for what it's worth—and at the considerable risk of hubris—years and even decades after I have given speeches or done consults, people often approach me to say, "Your statement about rediscovering my Deep Joy is the best advice I've ever gotten." So, I believe it just might be worth the effort . . .

With these thoughts concerning leadership and leading, we'll next turn to why "Leading Alone Is Worthless . . . But Leading Teams Is Priceless."

WHY LEADING IS PRICELESS SUMMARY

- Leadership is worthless . . . because it's a noun, the things you *say*—just words.
- But leading is priceless . . . because it's a verb, the actions you *do*—not just words.
- Think, act, and innovate—because the way we're working isn't working.
- Replace the passive, toxic word "Someday . . ." with the healing word "Today!"
- Everyone is a leader—lead yourself, lead your team—the leader you are looking for . . . is you!

2

TEAM WORK . . .
OR TEAMWORK

If you want to go fast, go alone.
If you want to go far, go together.

—MANDE AFRICAN PROVERB[1]

Relationships are what bond us together into highly functioning
teams, where each teammate is a leader. While the work *begins*
within, it *turns toward teamwork*. The art consists of changing the
hard slog of "Team *Work*" into the seamless, seemingly effortless art
of teamwork.

As an undergraduate theology major, I learned the value of con-
templative reflection and regeneration, now often called *mindfulness*.
As a football player, I learned the value of teamwork. And as a sports
medicine physician, I learned the value of performance, rest, and
recovery—both as an individual and as a team. All three are necessary to lead teams.

The Mande proverb quoted above reminds us that going far requires going together. During decades of leading in crisis, it has been
my experience that great leaders have all played on teams at some
point in their lives, at some level. By that I don't exclusively mean a

sports team, but teams of any kind, including cheerleading, dance teams, chess teams, debate teams, bands, orchestras, choirs, and many others. True loners rarely lead teams effectively, although plenty of introverts do. And to be clear, every family is a team, particularly happy families, as Tolstoy noted in the opening lines of *Anna Karenina*:

> *Every happy family is happy in the same way.*
> *Every unhappy family is unhappy in their own way.*[2]

Virtually every NFL team at some point before the game huddles up and chants, "Family on 3!" Similarly, work teams build on the foundation of family.

My friend Dr. Bob Waldinger is a psychiatrist, psychotherapist, Zen priest, and director of the world's longest and most in-depth study of happiness. This research project—The Harvard Study of Adult Development, originally known as the Glueck and Grant studies—followed 724 Harvard undergraduates and a group of working-class Boston men for more than 80 years, from young adulthood to old age, and is now studying their baby boomer children.[3]

According to the study, there is one single thing that predicts both the length and quality of the lives of the men from both groups: the number and quality of the relationships they have. That's a testament to teamwork since the most effective teams are built on a sturdy bedrock of relationships. Don't build resumes, build relationships.

DEFINING A TEAM

Teamwork requires a common understanding of what a team is. Throughout this book, I try to keep things as simple as possible and to assure that *definitions drive solutions,* by which I mean that the very act of defining a term should guide us to solving the issue being defined. Or as Einstein said, "Everything should be made as simple as possible, but no simpler."[4]

A team is simply two or more people who share a common purpose and work interdependently to attain that goal. Every team should share these four elements:

- A clear and inspired common sense of purpose—what is the "Why?"
- Deep and abiding respect among all team members—team spirit and respect.
- A shared system and processes to accomplish the clearly defined goals—a game plan.
- A culture of team success, guided by a deep commitment to mutual coaching and mentoring—success comes from coaching and mentoring.

While we commonly associate teams with sports or business organizations, all mutually interdependent actions are done in teams, whether formally described as such or not. For example, the most common, earliest, and most powerful teams we participate in are our families. Each team member brings their own unique skills, talents, abilities, background, and motivation to the family team's common purpose. A single mother is every bit as much a team leader as the CEO of a major international corporation. And every team requires the disciplines of teamwork.

THE DISCIPLINES OF TEAMWORK—FROM TEAM WORK TO TEAMWORK

Leading teams is a study in relationships. However, it is critical to understand that teamwork requires not only relationships, but is subject to the *disciplines of teamwork*, which are a set of skills required to build and sustain teamwork. Without these disciplines, it's team *work*, not teamwork. Leading teams requires work, to be sure, but it is impossible to attain and sustain without the tools of teamwork, which makes the "work" in teamwork infinitely easier and more effective.

In every team, including families, there are the *seams of the team*, the ways in which team members interact to form a disciplined and high-performance team. These include:

- The paradox of teamwork
- Hire right—A Team vs. B Team

- The role of re-recruitment
  - Re-recruit your A Team members every day.
  - Re-recruit your B Team members to coach and mentor them to the A Team.
  - Reconsider if the C Team members are on the right team and if they are willing to be coached and mentored. If not, bench them—or cut them from the team.
- Move from "My team" to "Our team"—a great litmus test for "Are you a team?" and even better for an A Team.
- The team is bigger than you think.
- Create a culture of continuous coaching and mentoring, and create that culture all day, every day.
- What to do when the team breaks down.

Let's take a closer look at each of these disciplines of teamwork.

THE PARADOX OF TEAMWORK

The power of teams is universal, unquestionable, and inevitable. But teamwork is even more powerful—and less well understood. As we move from leading to leading teams, it's important to point out an essential paradox, which is:

We can confidently assure those we serve that we will have a *team of experts* to serve them, but we can less confidently assure them that they will be taken care of by an *expert team*.

The original nine key characters of the hit show *ER* were conceived of as supremely smart and talented people. In NFL parlance, they would all "make the 53," meaning the 53-man roster comprising NFL teams. (Major League Baseball teams have 26-man rosters, the NBA and WNBA have 14-person rosters, and the US Women's National Soccer team has 23 superstars.)

In addition, all the *ER* cast members are very attractive, except for Dr. Mark Green, played by Anthony Edwards, who looks like me—except with a little bit of hair and glasses. (Full disclosure, I was a script consultant for the show *ER* for five years.)

We can confidently assure those we serve that we have a *team of experts* ...

But can we assure them we have *an expert team?*

Having a *team of experts* is not enough to assure success—it takes teamwork, delivered by a talented, *expert team.* In leading, don't just hire smart people—they can always be trained to get smarter as needed, and everyone needs to get smarter on different things to varying degrees at different times. Instead, hire *motivated* people who know that their Deep Joy intersects the world's deep needs on your team. Let their passion guide their learning and their character guide the way. Coach Bill Belichick was precise and correct in his advice:

Talent sets the floor of a team, but character sets the ceiling.[5]

Leading requires a ceiling set by the character of the people comprising the team. It is their character—and the Deep Joy informing that character—that drives their leading. The same is true of the ultimate team, the family. Family members seek to educate one another to become more expert in their knowledge, but it is character and the seams of the team that should be our first priority. And remember: Without seams, there is no team. Pay attention to the seams of the team—the nature and way team members interact. In focusing on the seams of the team, we eliminate what Phil Ensor in 1982 referred to as *functional silos.*[6]

TEAM COHESION IN A CRISIS

A struggling branch of a major bank had poor performance metrics and was plagued by turnover within its team. The branch was in a tough neighborhood and the staff were demoralized, particularly with rampant rumors that the branch was about to close, which meant they would lose their jobs. A friend of mine, a young, upcoming branch manager named Steve, was appointed to "turn the operation around."

Steve met with the branch's staff and immediately asked for every team member's resignation, after which they would be "allowed" to reapply for their jobs.

After the meeting, a bank employee, whose father was a US Navy veteran, tentatively knocked on the new manager's door then had a seat. After a moment, he asked Steve,

"Permission to speak freely, sir?"

"I suppose so," Steve hesitantly replied.

The bank employee then told my friend the following story:

On December 7, 1941, the Japanese fleet launched an attack on the US Pacific Fleet at Pearl Harbor on Oahu, virtually destroying the US ability to wage naval war in the Pacific theater. By all historical accounts, the attack could and should have been foreseeable, given the intelligence available at the time. But except for a few ships which were out to sea and a group of fighter bombers already launched on a training mission, the fleet was decimated, as the haunting memorial of the USS Arizona attests.

The employee continued, "Admiral Chester Nimitz was immediately dispatched to Pearl to command the Pacific Fleet. The officers were gathered to meet the new commander, fully expecting to be sacked. But Nimitz shook each man's hand, looked him in the eye and said, 'I have complete trust and faith in you. Now let's go win this war together!'"

After relating the Nimitz story to Steve, the bank employee simply rose from the chair and quietly walked out of the room.

The next morning, before the bank opened, Steve met with the team again and said, "Forget the resignations and reapplying for your jobs. I have complete trust and faith in you. Now let's go turn this branch around together!"

> Which, despite obstacles and a few setbacks, they pro-
> ceeded to do while keeping the team intact. And to put the ic-
> ing on the cake, the branch worked its way onto the Great
> Places to Work list.

If The Boss isn't willing to be a part of the team—and have the
character and humility to do so—they can never lead. And as C.S.
Lewis correctly noted:

> *Humility doesn't mean thinking less of yourself.*
> *But it does mean thinking of yourself less.*[7]

HIRE RIGHT—HIRE BADASSES

Facing significantly uncertain ground on our quest to keep our NFL
players safe, while navigating a path to safely playing NFL games during the COVID-19 crisis in early 2020, De Smith, executive director
of the NFLPA, instructed me to find the best possible experts across
the globe to act as a task force to advise and guide us with the best
science.

After we convened this group, Andrew Beaton, an excellent reporter for the *Wall Street Journal*, interviewed me about the process.
Andrew asked me about the qualifications of the members of the
group, and before I could take a moment to think, I said, "They're all
serious badasses!" What I meant was they were not only scientists, but
they had seen disasters many times before.

The next morning, May 27, 2020, the *Journal* headlines blared:

> *The Doctor and the Badasses Keeping NFL Players*
> *Safe from the Coronavirus*[8]

A significant part of "hire right" is to hire "badasses," people who
can truly say, "Been there, done that, got the T-shirt!"

When I was given the highest honor of the American College of
Emergency Physicians (and, yes, it was a slow year for nominees . . .),
I was asked the secret of my success, to which I replied:

> I have only one talent—I not only hired people who
> were better than me,
> I hired people who were *much* better than me.

Hire badass people who are better than you in any given area, and the entire team will benefit.

HIRE RIGHT TO LEAD—A TEAM VS. B TEAM

Every team has A Team members, B Team members, and C Team members (but hopefully no D or F Team members).[9] A Team members are the folks who, when you see them arriving at work, you think, "Yes! This team can take care of anything—it's going to be a great day." And chances are, it will be a great day.

However, when you see B or C Team members, you think, "Shoot me, shoot me, shoot me! I can't work with you—I worked with you last time. Who makes the schedule around here, anyway?" Every team member knows who the A, B, and C Team members are . . . except the B and C Team members . . .

Try this exercise: Ask your team to list the attributes of the A Team members, followed by the attributes of the B Team members. Across all teams, departments, and businesses this is what you will find, having done this exercise with more than 50,000 people over the years:

A TEAM MEMBERS

- Positive
- Proactive
- Confident
- Competent
- Compassionate
- Communication
- Teamwork
- Trust
- Teacher
- Does whatever it takes

- Sense of humor
- Gets things done

B TEAM MEMBERS

- Negative
- Reactive
- Poor communicator
- Lazy
- Late
- Constant complainer
- Can't do
- Always surprised
- BMW club

(For those unfamiliar with the term "BMW club," it stands for "bitch, moan, and whine"!)

"Hire right" means hiring—and continuously developing and promoting—those A Team attributes. Reward your A Team champions . . . and corral the B Team stragglers, whose negative, reactive attributes will otherwise infect and spread through the team.

RE-RECRUIT YOUR TEAM

When I was a pediatric surgical resident at the University of Utah, I met my beautiful and brilliant wife, Maureen, who was a neonatal intensive care flight nurse. Flight nurses are the baddest of the badass nurses in the extremely stressful neonatal intensive care unit, handling desperately ill, tiny humans and willing them to live.

One day, while skiing at Alta Ski Resort, we climbed above the normal runs to a chute called "Gunsight," named for the V-shaped rocks that framed it. In that spectacular setting, I asked Maureen to marry me, to which she readily agreed, but then told me, "Thom, I will marry you . . . but you have to 're-recruit' me every day of our marriage!"

I wasn't entirely sure what she meant by that, but I figured, "Hey if this brilliant woman will marry me, I'll figure it out over time." And I did, constantly re-recruiting her for the past 43 years . . .

We live amid The Great Resignation, a term coined by Anthony Klotz, an economics professor at Texas A&M University.[10] Many people are deciding to leave the jobs they have for others. (Perhaps ones that more closely approximate their "Deep Joy" . . .) They may not know what job they *want* to do, but they definitely know what job they *don't* want to do—the job they have. The workforce staffing-and-retention crisis is so severe that it constitutes the second pandemic for many businesses and across industries.

But there's an answer. The cure for The Great Resignation is . . . re-recruitment!

RE-RECRUIT YOUR A TEAM MEMBERS EVERY DAY

A Team members recruit new A Team members . . . But B Team members recruit C Team members, thinking it will make them look better—when it only makes the team perform worse. Thank your A Team members every day and every time you observe their excellence. Simple statements are powerful, such as, "Ann, you make this a better place every time you come to work—thanks!" Or "John, I saw how you handled that angry customer—you turned a raging tiger into a pussycat. Great job!"

And use the A Team members to coach and mentor new hires. Parents coach and mentor ceaselessly, like when saying, "Son that was a very tough loss, but we admire how you kept your head up and congratulated the other team, shaking every one of their hands."

RE-RECRUIT YOUR B TEAM MEMBERS TO COACH AND MENTOR THEM TO JOIN THE A TEAM

It's tempting to give up on B Team members, but most of them can cross over to the A Team with the right coaching—not from you, but from the A Team members. Let them know, "Kirk, I need your help. I believe in you and your potential to lead. So much so that I've asked Ann to work with you as a coach. As you know, she's one of our best."

LOOK IN THE MIRROR

When I speak to audiences about re-recruiting the B Team to join the A Team, I ask them two questions. First, I ask:

"When an A Team member looks in the mirror, what do they see?"

It's a bit of a trick question, because the answer they eventually come to is, "They see an A Team member." Humility notwithstanding, A Team members recognize precisely how they arrived at A Team behaviors—they work for the team and for those they serve.

The second question I ask is this:

"When a B Team member looks in the mirror, what do *they* see?"

The answer of course, is "An A Team member!" (Which makes me remark that B Team members are worse than vampires. At least vampires see nothing in the mirror—the B Team member sees an A Team visage looking back at them.)

So, what's the point?

First, no one is immune from this—as I've said many times when counseling others, "No one looks in the mirror and says, 'What a knucklehead!'" We all see what we want to see . . . which is an infinitely better image than our teammates see.

Second, leading requires us to hold the mirror up to the B Team members, showing them how their actions and behaviors affect others.

Third, suggest to them how their actions and behaviors might be changed to join the A Team.

Re-recruit the B Team members by holding up the mirror to them, showing them what their behavior is doing to both those we serve and the team itself.

When you start a sentence with "I need your help," you make it clear you need the cooperation for which you are asking—not many people will turn that down.

RECONSIDER YOUR C TEAM MEMBERS

As much as you might like the people who are on your C Team, you can't let them remain on that team for long—it's either up or out. Since everyone knows who the B and C Team members are, if you fail to deal with them and their caustic habits, your credibility as a leader is shot. In effect, you are telling the rest of the team they have to learn to deal with them, which means there are two sets of rules—one set for the A Team and another for the B and C Teams. Reconsider if the members of your C Team are on the right team and if they are willing to be coached and mentored. If not, then bench them—or cut them. It's just that simple.

Despite our best efforts, there will always be those who refuse to be coached and who don't really want to be a part of the team. This victim mentality is toxic to the team, your organization, your customers, and beyond. In addition to everything else we've talked about under the subject of leading so far, leading means corralling the stragglers and cutting them out of the herd when necessary. It's an important part of the job.

In every organization, there are always going to be some people who have simply misunderstood that their Deep Joy does not reside in the work they are currently doing, nor in the team they are on. Better to help them discover that and join another team where the fit is better. I guarantee that someday, they'll thank you for it as one door closes and the door leading them to their Deep Joy opens wide.

FROM "MY TEAM" TO "OUR TEAM"

All language has meaning, and all behavior has meaning. Leading requires the ability to do an *exegesis*—an unpacking of what the language and behavior *mean*. This language is important:

Don't just *say* team—*play* team!

It's not the slogan on the walls that are most important, but the actions in the halls, that should reflect leading teams effectively across the seams.

Leaders who use the term *my team* are at least using the language of teams. But the first-person possessive form connotes an authoritarian nature, as if the leader is the focus and not the team, which is where the proper emphasis should be. When I hear The Boss say, "My team," I can't help but think, "Wait, I thought it was *everyone's* team!" And it misses Gandhi's excellent point when he said:

> *There go my people. I am their leader. I must follow them.*[11]

"My team," while marginally better than "Me!" still misses the relationship nature of all effective teams. "Our team" much more effectively captures the nature of teams and teamwork. Tacitly, it invites team members to join and take mutual accountability, which is the only effective accountability in teams. Use the language and behaviors effectively and put them to use in leading every day.

For example, as an emergency physician, I believe passionately that all of us in healthcare need to not only make the patient a part of the team, but the most important part of the team. That starts when I make my first impression, which is the first time I walk into their room. Here's what I say:

> Hello Mrs. Smith, I am Doctor Mayer, a board-certified specialist in emergency medicine. Jody, your nurse, and I are leading an expert team of people who are honored to be a part of your care. When you talk with one of us, you are talking with all of us, since we communicate constantly on your behalf. But you are the most important part of our team—we are here to serve you. When you have questions or need additional information, please let us know. Without you, there is no "Us."

Regardless of what business you are in, you can use similar language to let those you serve know they are the most important team members of *our team*. And to those you serve, hearing, "Without you, there is no 'Us'" always produces a smile.

The same is true of a family. A mom creates, coaches, and leads a team known as the family—and the marriage. Her husband and her kids are teammates, who together create a seamless team. All teams are "our" team, not "my" team. As always, Shakespeare gets it perfectly right in the St. Crispin's Day speech in *Henry V*:

> *We few, we happy few—we band of brothers.*[12]

THE TEAM IS BIGGER THAN YOU THINK

In healthcare, as in many businesses and industries—and in some families, there is a term that is used too often and without consideration of what the language means. For example, we refer to the team members in certain areas of the hospital—including laboratory services, radiology, and housekeeping or environmental services (EVS)—as people who provide "_____ services." And when I ask a healthcare audience to fill in that blank, they invariably say "ancillary services."

What is the derivation of the word "ancillary"? I owe this insight to one of my Latin scholar sons, who told me it derives from the Latin *ancilla,* which translated literally means "female slave"!

Ancillary services—are we serious? How could a word's meaning be more insulting and demeaning? Please stop using that term—*immediately.* Start calling these team members what they truly are—*essential* services. We cannot work without them, and they are essential to our lives.

Raise your children with this wisdom and teach them to thank everyone they meet, including bussers, teachers, coaches, trainers, and all the other people who are there to help. (And as we'll see, thank yous are infectious.)

There are no unimportant people on a team, as my story about Dr. White later in this chapter illustrates.

MOST VALUABLE TEAMMATE

I first met Tom Brady years ago, when De Smith (then the executive director of the NFLPA), Eric Winston, our president, Sean Sansiveri, and I had the chance to speak with him over a three-hour period. Great athletes who lead their teams are the first to say it's the team, not the individual that counts, and it's teams, not individuals, who win championships.

Tom Brady won seven Super Bowls in his 22-year career and played with many great teammates, including Rob Gronkowski, Julian Edelman, Adam Vinatieri, Matthew Slater, Vince Wilfork, and Devin McCourty. But Tom is quick to say that the team member who was most responsible for the length of his career never played a snap in the NFL—indeed, never made a 53-man roster for any of his teams, because he wasn't a football player. His name is Alex Guerrero, and the title on his business card—under the logo of Tom's company, TB12—simply says, "Body Coach."

Some of the most influential (and best-paid) coaches on every team's staff are the strength and conditioning coaches, each of whom runs the program in the extensive weight rooms in the NFL. Most weight rooms are massive and the programs the strength coach designs are specifically devised to add muscle mass and strengthen the players to the maximum extent possible. Physiologically, this results in muscle fibers that collectively shorten and strengthen the muscle groups.

But as he worked with Alex, Tom came to learn that a quarterback's muscles only need a certain amount of strength and that his time—and his career—were better spent "lengthening and loosening" the throwing muscles as opposed to shortening and strengthening them.

The first time I met with Tom at any length was when he was still with the Patriots, in the TB12 offices 400 yards from Foxboro Stadium and the Patriots' training facilities. There he and Alex explained that as a team captain, Tom felt he needed to be seen working out with his teammates, following the plan. (Coach Bill Belichick certainly felt that way . . .) But after finishing the workouts, Tom met with Alex for hours at TB12, where, in effect, the process of reversing what was done in the training facility occurred, systematically and methodically.

A 22-year career is unusual for any NFL player, but nearly unheard of for a modern quarterback. Without his teammate, Alex, it might not have happened. Tom is the GOAT (Greatest of All Time), but he's the first to say that Alex is his MVT—Most Valuable Teammate.[13]

Performance, rest, and recovery is a cycle through which we all must go. But there are more than just the traditional ways to rest and recover . . . the team is bigger than you think, and there are no unimportant team members. Without his "Body Coach," Tom is the first to say his career would not have been as long . . . nor as successful.

I love my job as medical director of the NFLPA—the union for NFL players. In part, it is where my Deep Joy meets the world's deep needs. But we are a union of players—we exist for one purpose: to serve our players, their wives, their children, and often their parents. (Particularly during Covid . . .)

I often say I am the only doc I know who has more than 10,000 patients. But I am only a part of Team Health and Safety for our players. Sean Sansiveri has been my copilot and legal partner for 14 years, Dr. Sid Hinds joined us as deputy medical director and chief health equity officer last year, and Don Davis and his fellow player directors— who are the voice of the player-patient in the locker rooms of the teams to which they are assigned—are all part of Team Health and Safety for the NFLPA. Together, all of us serve our 2,500 player-patients, our president JC Tretter, and our executive director, Lloyd Howell.

The team is always bigger than you think!

LEADING MEANS CREATING A CULTURE OF MUTUAL COACHING AND MENTORING

Super Bowl LI was played between the Atlanta Falcons and the New England Patriots at NRG Stadium in Houston on February 5, 2017. It is widely known as "The 28–3 Game," because the Patriots overcame a deficit of that magnitude to win the game in the first Super Bowl to go to overtime. How did they do that?

Many people assume that it was Tom Brady, the GOAT, who was responsible for the comeback. Others point to coach Bill Belichick as the master of halftime adjustments—which he definitely is. But the true architect of the comeback was a 67-year-old offensive line coach for the Patriots named Dante Scarnecchia, or "Coach Scar," as he is affectionately known by his players. (Scar's area of the Patriots practice field was less affectionately called "Dante's Inferno" . . .) Coach Scar always taught his offensive linemen that the most important key to their offensive line's team success was a brutally simple tactic:

Thumbs up, fingers out!

Please do that for me now as you read. You will see that executed correctly, this move requires you to pull your elbows into your sides. Coach Scar told the linemen at halftime they had forgotten that principle and let their thumbs rotate in, which forces the elbows up and out—creating a huge lever for the defensive linemen and edge rushers. And that's exactly why the Falcons' rushers had been able to pressure Tom Brady so effectively, resulting in only 3 points in the first half.

As Archimedes said, "Give me a lever long enough and I can move the world."[14] The Patriots offensive line created a lever for the Falcons throughout the first half of the game. In the second half, however—after Coach Scar's feedback—they reverted to their (good) old habits. As a result, the Falcons had a difficult time getting to the quarterback, giving him plenty of time to throw—and completing the biggest comeback in Super Bowl history.

When you coach, coach details . . . Details matter.

The same principle should be at work in all our leading by creating a culture of mutual coaching and mentoring, where each team member is both open to being coached and mentoring—and equally willing to coach and mentor others. The Irish poet Derek Mahon captures this well in his poem "Everything Will Be Alright":

The poems flow
From the hand unbidden
And the hidden source
Is a watchful heart.[15]

In creating and sustaining a culture of mutual coaching and mentoring, the details of a watchful heart are important. When asked what to say in a speech or writing, I give the same advice: Open your heart and you will find the answers you seek. One of those answers in leading teams is the skill of gratitude.

The first of three habits of the watchful heart is realizing there is *never anyone* who can do "nothing for you." Everyone on every team is important.

The second is that we should all say "Thank you" at least 50 times per day—that's a habit worth developing and curating in leading teams . . . because "Thank you" is infectious. When you are generous with your thanks, your entire team will develop the habit and the team will be stronger for it.

The third is to make it easy to "harvest compliments," which I understand sounds a bit odd. Everyone knows about complaint departments and the idea of service recovery when things go wrong. Start catching people doing things right, harvest those compliments, and feed them back to the ones who created those experiences by leading in their actions.

A watchful heart does all three of those things, consistently and with love and generosity for all.

WISDOM IN AN NFL LOCKER ROOM

As a part of my duties as the medical director for the NFLPA, Sean Sansiveri and I visit different NFL training camps each year. During these visits, we meet with the players, but also the team physicians, trainers, and coaches. Several years ago, we visited the Denver Broncos' training camp, and I noticed a sign with the Broncos' logo at the bottom, which is above each door leaving the locker room and training facility. It reads:

You can easily judge the character of a man by how he treats those who can do nothing for him.

As you may know, that quote is from the German philosopher, Wolfgang Goethe. I asked the head athletic trainer, Steve "Greek" Antonopulos about the sign and he said,

Oh, Coach (Gary) Kubiak feels very strongly about that quote, which his father always told him.

The wisdom of Goethe in an NFL locker room . . .

DR. WHITE AND IMPORTANT PEOPLE

I went to college to play football and didn't even know what a "major" was. I chose a major in theology because I was interested in the nature of the world and why people acted the way they do. (And, candidly, because you only had to write papers, not take tests . . .) At the end of my sophomore year, Dr. Gordon Campbell, my theology adviser, and Dr. Enos Pray, who taught a required biology course I had taken, took me to lunch and asked me a question:

Has it ever occurred to you that you might have more impact as a doctor instead of a theologian?

I had no earthly idea what a doctor was—wasn't that the guy who sewed up my face when I got a laceration? (Or who stuck his finger in an uncomfortable place and told me to cough during my football physical?) But since I trusted them, I thought, "Why not? Let's give it a whirl."

As a result, I had to start taking premed courses in my junior year that undergraduate students hoping to go to medical school usually took in their freshman year. I started with Chemistry 101, taught by Dr. Keith White, the chair of the Chemistry Department. It went fine, if not well, until the first exam, which consisted of 100 questions. I opened the test and read the first question:

A mole is Avogadro's number of particles or _____

There were five answers, A through E. Now, I had no idea who Avogadro was, much less why he had a number, or what it was. A mole? Isn't that a critter?

Since I had no clue, I thought, "Well, this has been fun—back to theology for me. Is it too late to drop this course?" But I took a guess, deciding, since I was clueless, that I would answer each question in sequence: ABCDE, EDCBA, and so on through all 100 questions. (In football, one of the routes a receiver runs is called a "slant and go" route, where the receiver first angles across the field and then breaks off and heads straight up field. We call it a "sluggo route.")

My answer sheet looked like a series of successive sluggo routes. But at the end of the test there was a blue envelope on which was written, "BONUS QUESTION—If you get this question right, you will get an A on this test, regardless of your score on the first 100 questions."

How bad can this be, I thought. At least it's not Avogadro . . .

I opened the envelope, removing and unfolding the piece of paper, which read:

What's the name of the man who cleans this room every night so you can have a great place to learn?

I walked up to Dr. White's desk—I was the first one done since it doesn't take long to finish a test when you don't read the questions . . .

I tentatively began, "Dr. White, this bonus question . . ."

He smiled and nodded yes.

"Do you want his first name or his last name?" I asked.

Dr. White took off his glasses and pointed to me. "Thom, if you can give me his first and last name, I will not only give you an A on this test, I'll give you an A in this course, as long as you show up and do the work."

Emboldened, I asked one more question. "What if I can also give you his wife's name and the names and ages of his six children?"

Dr. White stood up and said, "Thom, if you can do *that*, I'll not only give you an A in this course, I will give you an A in every chemistry course I teach, as long as you show up and do the work!"

I was as good as my word, and he was as good as his.

The point? I became a doctor not because of my inherent intelligence or intellect . . .

But because of a janitor at my school . . .

Remember: There are *no* unimportant people . . .

After I tell this story, I am often asked how it was that I knew the janitor and his family so well. The answer is that I didn't even get to the chemistry lab until after the school day, football practice, and finishing my theology essays. So, Roosevelt Richmond—the school janitor—and I got there about the same time and talked every night about life, his family, including his wife and kids, and his day job. When he saw me there at school in the midnight hour, he always said, "There he is! He's got fire in the belly!"

Actually, I just didn't plan my time all that well . . . and I had infinite curiosity for him to share his wisdom. I stayed in touch with Roosevelt after graduation, medical school, and residency—until he passed away. And I owe my MD degree to him.

WHAT TO DO WHEN THE TEAM BREAKS DOWN

Despite our best efforts at leading teams, there are inevitably times when the team breaks down. What can we do when that happens?

- Look for the seams of the team—that's usually where problems develop.
- Move to the other side—state the problem from the other team members' perspective, not yours.
- Reconnect to the team's Deep Joy and passion.
- Look for outliers who have strayed from the team.
- Don't be afraid to call an audible, changing the play but not the vision and the Deep Joy to which the team has committed.

The work begins within . . . but it turns toward teamwork. That's why leading alone is a necessary, but not a sufficient condition for leading. It takes a team.[16]

In the next chapter, we will explore why leading teams requires innovation at the speed of trust.

TEAM WORK . . . OR TEAMWORK SUMMARY

- A team of experts is not an expert team.
- Hire right. Don't hire smart, hire Deep Joy and passion.
- The team is bigger than you think—there are no unimportant team members.
- Say "thank you" 50 times a day and harvest compliments, not just complaints.

3

INNOVATION AT THE SPEED OF . . . TRUST

Ever tried. Ever failed. No matter. Try again. Fail again. Fail better.

SAMUEL BECKETT[1]

Not long into my tenure as the NFLPA's first medical director, I faced a difficult issue with which I felt I needed our executive director Gene Upshaw's help. The issue was important enough that I took the unusual step of making an appointment at NFLPA headquarters with him to discuss it. Soon after the meeting started, I asked Gene which of the three possible solutions that I had formulated he thought I should pursue to resolve this thorny problem.

Gene looked at me and said, "Just go be Thom Mayer. That's why you are Thom Mayer. That's why I hired Thom Mayer."

After I walked out of Gene's office, I immediately called my wife, Maureen. She asked, "What did Gene say?"

"I don't have a clue!" was my befuddled reply.

Looking back, I now know exactly what Gene was saying to me that day. Although he didn't utter the "T" word—*trust*—that's exactly the message he meant to convey to me. When he told me, "Just go be Thom Mayer," Gene was communicating to me that he trusted my judgment and that's why he made the decision to hire me in the first place. And as of that moment, I hadn't done anything that would negatively affect that impression.

So, I say to you, "Just go be yourself, guided by your Deep Joy and trusting that if you open your heart and lead by serving others, you will prevail in the long run."

Trust yourself! Trust others!

Because innovation occurs at the speed of trust.

INNOVATION AT THE SPEED OF TRUST

Every leader in every organization says that they want their people to innovate, but why? Precisely because the way we're working . . . isn't working. So, innovation is a necessity, not a luxury. But while innovation requires some degree of intellect, intelligence, and creativity, it can only flourish in an environment deeply infused with trust. And few things are more toxic to innovation than distrust.

I have spoken to many world-class organizations about innovation, and when I ask about the success rate of those innovations, they often proudly proclaim something along the lines of, "We've done the math, and 95 percent of our innovations are successful!"

My standard response is, "If 95 percent of your innovations are successful, then you aren't really innovating—you're playing it safe."

The thing is, any organization with a 95 percent innovation success rate is an organization that lacks the trust necessary for its people to feel comfortable taking risks and occasionally failing in doing so.[2] This is a really important distinction for every leader to keep in mind, so we'll dig deeper into it in the next chapter. As Beckett says, "Fail better." And my great friend and management thinker Tom Peters says, "Fail forward faster. Punish mediocre successes. Reward excellent failures."[3]

To innovate, a team's members need to feel they have the trust of their leaders and are fully empowered to follow their Deep Joy and the team's mutual vision. Most innovation teams don't tear down an existing system and replace it with a new one. They instead make small changes *within* a system, tinkering around the edges without radically changing what needs to be changed. This isn't good enough when it comes to creating real innovation—the kind of innovation that will move your organization forward.

When Gallup surveyed 10,000 people to find out what things leaders must give their employees so they will "feel engaged and connected to their organization and their day-to-day work," the following words were used most often: compassion, stability, hope—and *trust*.[4] One of your most important jobs as a leader is to show the people who work for and with you that you trust them implicitly.

To know that you are trusted and appreciated is perhaps second in importance in life only to the knowledge that you are loved. There is no substitute for it as we face the daunting challenge of leading in crisis by innovating new and creative ways of working and living.

TRUSTING THE DOCTOR

One sunny Saturday afternoon in late February 2009, while standing on the sideline watching our son Kevin's Duke lacrosse team warm up for their game at Koskinen Stadium, my cell phone rang, playing the "Pink Panther Theme" I set for my ringtone. Not recognizing the number, I answered as I always do, "This is Dr. Mayer, tell me how I can help you." A voice I did not recognize said, "Doc, this is DeMaurice Smith. You don't know me, but I am one of the candidates for executive director for the NFLPA. Do you have a few minutes to talk?"

"Of course!" I replied. "I would be happy to help in any way that I can." De explained that a central part of his strategy for the players' union was to include key health and safety issues in the looming collective bargaining agreement (CBA). De wanted to know my thoughts and specifically if I would agree to become the first physician ever directly involved in CBA negotiations in any sport.

Thus began a 15-year relationship that changed the entire culture of concussion, while elevating how the short- and long-term issues of health and safety would be addressed in sports forever. De's fierce leadership and his trust in me to be, as he says, "a junk yard dog" to get the right things done for our players resulted in a massive paradigm shift that has rippled through the world of contact sports.

Today this ripple continues to expand into all football injuries and other aspects of sports medicine. But it all started with a leader's trust in someone—me—to do something that had never been done before . . .

The very fact that the way we're working isn't working means we need to innovate new ways, better ways that reconnect us to our Deep Joy. *Innovation is not a luxury—it is a necessity.* Many people attribute a quote from the novelist Rita Mae Brown to Einstein (who never said it and whose biographer, Walter Isaacson, assured me that was the case):

> *One definition of insanity is to keep doing the same thing over and over again, but expecting different results.*[5]

Innovation at the speed of trust is critical whenever we expect different, improved results.

Coach Lou Holtz is one of the greatest coaches in collegiate football history, including 10 years at the University of Notre Dame. After his first year on the job there, his teams were never ranked lower than fifth in the nation. Yet in 1996, Lou suddenly retired, walking away from a lifetime contract. But three years later, Lou returned to the collegiate ranks as head coach at the University of South Carolina.

One day I asked him a question that had been on my mind for a long time: "Coach, why did you retire from Notre Dame?"

"Doc, it's the strangest thing," he told me. "We took Notre Dame to a national championship in my second year and had great success every year after that. But of course, our boosters thought we should have won every year. I retired from Notre Dame because I thought I was tired of coaching. I came back to South Carolina, because I realized I wasn't tired of coaching—I was tired of maintaining!"

Leading by maintaining is exhausting work. Innovation is a cure for maintaining, whether in coaching or in life. But innovation requires thinking in creative, sometimes crazy ways, some of which will fail.

GET CRAZY

My senior thesis in college was on Thomas Kuhn's book *The Structure of Scientific Revolutions*, which described the concept of paradigm shifts.[6] When I researched the topic, the following story had a deep impact on my thinking.

During the late 1950s the science of physics was what biotechnology has become today—the area where the best and most elite minds of science gravitated, as exciting developments concerning the nature of the universe unfolded. In 1958 at Columbia University, the greatest minds in physics (except Einstein, who was at Princeton that day) gathered to present the most cutting-edge concepts. Wolfgang Pauli rose to present his unified field theory, intended to tie together Newtonian mechanics, quantum mechanics, Einstein's General and Special Theories of Relativity, and Heisenberg's uncertainty principle—an ambitious goal to be sure. When he finished, Niels Bohr, widely considered the only physicist in a class with Einstein, stood at the dais to discuss the paper. Gazing at Pauli, he said, "We all agree that your theory is crazy. The question which divides us is is it crazy enough to have a chance at being correct?"[7]

My question to you is this:

"Are *you* crazy enough to admit that the way we're working isn't working and to innovate new, cutting-edge ways of doing things differently?"

Because anyone must be a bit crazy to admit that to live in this world, we need to reinvent this world and the systems and processes in which we labor. You must have a "crazy streak" to dream impossible ways of doing things differently and then make them possible. My advice is if you aren't "crazy enough" . . .

Go get crazy!

FLOW AND INNOVATION

Embedded in the concept that innovation occurs at the speed of trust is a simple, yet penetrating question:

Who, of necessity, must "get crazy" to innovate
a new system?

Hold that thought for a moment as I note that, several years ago my business partner, Dr. Kirk Jensen, and I wrote a book titled *Hardwiring Flow: Systems and Processes for Seamless Patient Care.*[8] Building upon the seminal work of the great psychologist Mihaly Csikszentmihalyi, who wrote *Flow: The Psychology of Optimal Experience,*[9] we defined flow as two simple concepts regarding the systems and processes in which we work:

Hardwiring Flow means:

1. Stop doing stupid stuff
2. Start doing smart stuff

Since the way we're working isn't working (stop doing stupid stuff), the current work needs to be "fixed" by better systems and processes (start doing smart stuff.) To return to the previous point, the people who need to get crazy are the same people who will of necessity identify both the "stupid stuff" and the "smart stuff." This means—*you*, and anyone else who does the work and is forced to suffer through the very systems and processes that are burning everyone out. The Boss can't do it for you—even if they want or demand it. The Boss doesn't do the work you do and so cannot innovate for you— only the people who do the work can effectively retool the work.

That realization is precisely why innovation occurs at the speed of trust, where everyone is empowered to get crazy, identify and eliminate stupid stuff, and innovate and execute smart stuff. (And speaking of execution, the first coach of the expansion team Tampa Bay Buccaneers was John McKay. The Bucs had a horrible team, a horrible record, and had just played a horrible game. A reporter asked Coach McKay what he thought of his team's execution and his immediate response was, "I'm in favor of it!"[10])

INNOVATION, TRUST, AND INTRINSIC MOTIVATION

Abraham Maslow, best known for his description of the hierarchy of needs, is equally deserving of acclaim for the wisdom that all meaningful and lasting change is intrinsically motivated.[11]

"Do it because The Boss says so!" is extrinsic motivation, while "Do it because it makes your job easier and the lives of those we serve better" is intrinsic motivation. When you want to uncover the source of someone's intrinsic motivation, put your finger on the pulse of their *why*.

When leading innovation workshops on customer service, I ask the audience to fill in the blank in this sentence:

The #1 reason to innovate customer service is _____

I've gotten the widest possible range of answers in response to this exercise, but these are the most common:

- It's better for the patients/customer.
- It's better for the family.
- It's better for market share.
- Its' better for quality.
- It's better for branding.
- It's better for loyalty.

While all those things (and others) are true, it misses the true #1 reason for innovating customer service, which is . . . it makes our jobs easier, while making the lives of those we serve better.

The single best motivating *why* in life is that it makes your life easier and the lives of your customers better—otherwise, why do it? As German philosopher Friedrich Nietzsche explained, "He who has a strong enough 'why' can bear almost any 'how.'"[12] (Simon Sinek breathed new life into Nietzsche's insight with a popular TEDx talk and subsequent book *Start with Why.*[13]) Making your life easier, while making the lives of those you serve better is perhaps the ultimate *intrinsic motivation.*

And the same is true for innovation. Innovation should make your job easier, while making the lives of those you serve better. This is true, whether you are a CEO, homemaker, janitor, gardener, plumber, doctor, or nurse. Make sure you get the "why" before the "how" as you innovate at the speed of trust.

THINKING OUTSIDE THE BOX

Leading through action must be guided by trust—the trust that we are all human and subject to both success and failure. Only those who always color safely inside the lines are immune from failure, but who wants to live that way?

I advise caution when you hear The Boss say, "Think outside the box," because in my experience, what they really mean is, "Think inside *my* box!" Trying to discover what box The Boss is thinking of and endlessly trying to break out of it doesn't allow you to think outside *your* box.

I understand that many of us work in hierarchical organizations where The Boss calls the shots. In those cases, it's wise to invest some time in gaining insight into how and what that person thinks and through what lens they view the world. How do they make decisions? What guides them? But don't simply try to guess what box they are thinking of. To innovate, add your insights to how The Boss thinks when she innovates.

The first thing I say to people who seek my advice is, "Amaze me, educate me, and enlist me." By "amaze," I mean blow me way with a crazy, amazing idea. "Educate me" so I can get smarter about your idea. Then "enlist me" by telling me how I can help you with your amazing idea.

INNOVATION, TRUST, AND THE RIGHT PLACE

Without question, the work of innovation can be frustrating as failures multiply in the search for better ways of doing things. So much so that you may wonder if you are on track or even in the right place.

Two weeks into our deployment to Ukraine, while preparing to saddle up with the team and head out to see patients, the air raid sirens suddenly blared. I was in my dorm room on the second floor and heard the roar of three Ukrainian Su-27 Flanker jets as they flew by at eye level, followed by four Russian rockets. The rockets impacted just three blocks from where I was standing, breaking the windows in my room.

As I rushed outside and ran to help, I could see the thick black smoke rising into the sky from the rockets' impact. Later, when I returned to the United States, Pamela Brown of CNN asked me during a live interview, "What did you think when that happened?!"

I calmly replied, "I thought, 'I'm in the right place.'"[14]

Are you in the right place?

If you have identified your Deep Joy and followed and stayed true to it, and if you trust yourself and your team—you are *definitely* in the right place . . .

INNOVATION, BURNOUT, AND ADAPTIVE CAPACITY

To innovate, you and your team need something in addition to trust. You need *adaptive capacity*—that is, the *resilience*—to innovate.

My good friend Christina Maslach deserves immense credit for her description of the syndrome that plagues so many of us—burnout. For more than 30 years, she and her colleague Michael Leiter have plumbed the depths of burnout, culminating in their recent work *The Burnout Challenge*,[15] the draft of which I was honored to review and comment upon. (I highly recommend this book to anyone who wants to lead in the active voice.)

It did not take a global pandemic—caused by a tremendously destructive virus that disrupted our lives in so many ways—to create in our society an appreciation for the phenomenon of burnout, but it certainly put it on the front burner. Burnout knows no borders, affecting people in every organization, in every position, but to varying degrees. And while burnout rates differ by industry and job type, they are consistently among the highest in healthcare, with doctors and nurses leading a race they would prefer not to be in: the Burnout Sweepstakes.

Within my own specialty of emergency medicine, 60 percent of doctors and 50 percent of nurses have at least one symptom of burnout.[16] But no job is immune from this ailment. According to a recent survey conducted by Future Forum, 43 percent of US desk workers reported feeling burned out, with female employees reporting 32 percent more symptoms of burnout than males. Perhaps most surprising, 49 percent of 18-to-29-year-old workers reported feeling burned out versus 38 percent of employees who were 30 or older.[17]

In their book, Christina Maslach and Michael Leiter explained that employees who experience burnout typically exhibit this triumvirate of symptoms:

- Emotional exhaustion
- Cynicism
- Loss of meaning at work

They go on to say that burnout is particularly destructive for the people who suffer its effects: "Burnout is an apt term, suggesting a once-hot fire that has been reduced to ashes; those ashes are the feelings of exhaustion left after an initial flame of dedication and passion is extinguished."

Of course, no leader wants those outcomes. But if you say to your team:

- "Don't be so exhausted."
- "Don't be so cynical."
- "Don't be ineffective . . ."

. . . don't be surprised if your words frustrate and exasperate them. What are they supposed to do with *that?* They are already burned out—now they're even more burned out with no specific advice or direction for exactly how to get back to a less stressed state of mind. As a physician, I can tell you that you can't cure burnout—or any disease—by only addressing the symptoms—you've got to do something about the cause.

The burnout epidemic is of great personal concern to me, both for its negative effects on people, and for its toxic effects on organizations and families. So much so that I was privileged to contribute a book to the cause of fighting this epidemic titled, *Battling Healthcare Burnout: Learning to Love the Job You Have While Creating the Job You Love.*[18] I wrote the book because I realized that many definitions of burnout and its resolution were too lengthy, complex, and complicated. While the book was written about burnout in healthcare professionals, its lessons apply to anyone in any walk of life.

During my many years leading organizations I have found that "definitions drive solutions." Therefore, the very definition of a concept should not only be succinct, terse, clear, and straightforward, but should also provide the means to resolve the problem. In that spirit, I offer this definition of burnout:

$$\text{Burnout} = \frac{\text{Job Stressors}}{\text{Adaptive Capacity or Resilience}}$$

Burnout is simply a ratio of job stressors divided by the resilience or adaptive capacity of the individual to deal with those stressors.

So, how do you reduce burnout? It's simple. You either reduce job stressors or increase adaptive capacity/resilience or preferably you do both simultaneously. That requires innovation for both the numerator and the denominator. The mismatch in this ratio is precisely what causes the triumvirate of symptoms described by Christina Maslach and Michael Leiter: emotional exhaustion, cynicism, and alienation at work.

A quick cautionary note about the term "resilience"—it can sometimes have an unintended pejorative meaning. For example, if you say, "Our team is burned out because it lacks resilience," you're unconsciously sending the message, "You are burned out because you are not resilient enough." So, for the burned-out individual, their immediate, if unspoken, reaction is:

> *Are you kidding me? I'm the problem?!? You put me in this crazy system with all these stressors and you tell me I'm the problem?!?*

For that and many other reasons, I prefer to use the term "adaptive capacity" instead of "resilience" when I speak to people about burnout, although they ultimately mean the same thing.

I played football for most of my formative years, from the third grade through college and I had brief tryouts with the Bears and the Vikings. (The coaches advised me that I would be a great NFL player except I lacked one critical quality . . . talent!) I was very fortunate as a first-year college student to start as the middle linebacker, also known as the "Mike" linebacker, which was very unusual in those ancient days. Most Mike linebackers were experienced upper-level class athletes.

During the walk-through before our first game, we were all in our respective positions, in a pro-style 4-3 defense (which would now be called "Tampa 2," after Coach Tony Dungy's Super Bowl-winning formation). In the middle of the walk-through, the defensive coordinator suddenly shouted, "Mayer, my linebackers are Agile, Mobile, and Hostile! Is that you?" I responded, "Coach, I am all those things—I am agile, mobile, and hostile. But I am the middle linebacker, the Mike. I have to read and react—I have to adapt, adapt, adapt constantly."

Coach paused and said, "My linebackers are agile, mobile, hostile . . . and <u>adaptile</u>!"

As the burnout epidemic continues to gain ground, we must all be "adaptile"—developing, nourishing, and increasing our adaptive capacity for innovation to deal with the rising job stressors we face. So regardless of whether you use the term *adaptive capacity* or *resilience*, be ready to change to meet your job's and your organization's needs. Leading requires the ability to instill and nurture adaptive capacity in the entire team.

Helping your team build and develop their adaptive capacity is accepted *much* more easily than telling them they are not resilient enough. How you coach matters.

8 RULES FOR BUILDING THE TRUST YOU NEED TO INNOVATE

Most of us learned early in life the adage that trust takes *years* to build and only *seconds* to destroy. The fleeting and evanescent nature of

ADAPTIVE CAPACITY IN THE NFL

My friend Dr. Don Davis ("Triple D" or "D3") is the senior director, Player Affairs for the NFLPA, responsible for guiding five other player directors, who are all former NFL players with years of experience. Their job is to represent the voice of the player-patients in the NFL locker rooms for our union.

Don knows more about the "voice of the locker room" than anyone in football. It requires many talents, not the least of which is tremendous adaptive capacity. He comes by that from an 11-year playing career in the NFL for four teams and coaches, winning two Super Bowl rings. Following that, he became a strength and conditioning coach for the Patriots.

That last transition required a huge adaptation, as he says, "When you trade a helmet for a hat." Suddenly instead of being one of the guys you become one of the guys telling the guys what to do. Without a huge dose of adaptive capacity, he could never have pulled it off . . . but he did.[19]

trust is universal, but we must lead by building trust in our people, organizations, and families. Our ability to innovate and create depends on it.

Here are eight rules for building trust that I have found to be especially effective:

RULE 1: BE CONSTANTLY CONSISTENT

Consistency matters and it should be your constant focus, a firm foundation for all your relationships and especially your interactions. Always ask yourself before you act, "Will this build trust or break trust?" If it's going to break trust, don't do it.

Say what you are going to do. Do it!

Is it really that simple? You bet it is!

RULE 2: DO NOT BE AFRAID TO MAKE PROMISES—BE AFRAID TO BREAK THEM

Some people are so paranoid about abusing trust that they become afraid of making promises. Don't be that person. Instead, go out of your way in all your interactions to promise, but only on those things you can actually deliver.

RULE 3: UNDERPROMISE, OVERDELIVER

While making promises is important, so is being relatively conservative in what you promise. And if you are taking a risk with your promise, let the team know that. When you overdeliver, others trust you even more, which is like compound interest, it grows exponentially.

RULE 4: USE DEEP JOY AS YOUR NORTH STAR FOR TRUST

In every action, think, "Does this fit with my Deep Joy in the process of building trust?" If not, don't do it.

DEEP JOY IN WOMEN'S SOCCER

On March 17, 1972, a young girl was born in Selma, Alabama, who had a congenital orthopedic deformity known as *talipes equinovarus*, better known by its common, if unfortunate, name of "club foot," where the foot turns downward and inward. Without treatment, it is a disabling condition, but fortunately her parents immediately sought medical help and she was placed first in a cast and then in corrective shoes for a year.

As her mother said, "Once those came off, she started running—and she never stopped running." She ran so well and so fast that it became apparent to her parents and everyone else that she had an amazing talent for soccer. Throughout her youth, she ran and kept on running, but also honed her skills to the point that she was recruited to the University of North Carolina's women's soccer team by its famed coach, Anson Dorrance, where she led the team to an unprecedented four National Championships. At 15, she became the youngest player on the US Women's National Team.

By the time she retired in 2004, she was third on the list of most goals scored in international competition and had been part of the US's first World Cup title in 1991, as well as leading the "Dream Team" that won the 1999 World Cup over China in a shootout at the Rose Bowl in front of 90,000 people and with millions watching worldwide.

She told me, "For me it was always the joy of playing the game that drove me—that joy sustained me through all the sacrifices. But I also wanted to make sure that, no matter how bad a day I had or how badly I felt, I never let that pull my teammates down."

Her name, of course, is Mia Hamm and she remains a legend because her Deep Joy powered through a congenital deformity, as well as countless adversities along the way.

Follow your Deep Joy and trust in the path!

RULE 5: SHINE THE SPOTLIGHT ON OTHERS

When your teams deliver what was promised, make sure you reinforce the power of trust through language that shines a spotlight on the work you have done together. Simple words like, "It was great to work together on that project—we delivered!"

RULE 6: FREELY ADMIT MISTAKES

Don't be afraid to admit mistakes and your role in them. While "I'm sorry" are two of the most powerful words in the world, some people haven't been taught how to say them. (In my experience, males seem to have more trouble with this than females . . .) When our sons were younger, I would fix them breakfast and have them practice these magic words, "I'm sorry, I was wrong, it will never happen again."

One day, someone overheard our routine and said, "But they don't really mean it."

"No," I replied, "but when they do mean it, at least they will know how to say it." Some people can't seem to get the two simple words out of their mouths without choking on them . . .

RULE 7: BE KIND TO EVERYONE, INCLUDING YOURSELF

When Henry James's nephew Billy was heading off to Harvard, he asked his uncle for advice. James said, "The first is to be kind. The second is to be kind. And the third is to be always kind."[20] Follow that advice, but also be kind to yourself, forgive yourself when necessary, and remember, you are a performance athlete—invest in yourself.

RULE 8: DISAPPOINTMENT IS NORMAL, BUT GUILT AND BLAME ARE NOT

Things don't always work out with innovation—hence the need for trust. It's OK to be disappointed—as long as you use the power of that emotion to fuel future innovation. But blame and guilt are toxic. To move forward, find a cleaner-burning fuel than guilt. And remember, innovation always involves the risk of failure—which just happens to be the subject of the next chapter.

INNOVATION AT THE SPEED OF . . . TRUST SUMMARY

- Innovation is a necessity in today's organizations—not just a desirable option—and it occurs at the speed of trust.
- Fail better. Fail forward faster.
- Burnout is just a ratio of work stressors divided by adaptive capacity or resiliency.
- Burnout is the inability to fully experience your Deep Joy.

4

MAKING FAILURE
YOUR FUEL

*I didn't invent the incandescent light bulb. I invented
1,000 ways not to invent an incandescent light bulb.*

—THOMAS ALVA EDISON[1]

When I was a pediatric surgical resident, at the end of each rotation,
I would meet with the chief of the service in her office and ask a simple
question:

What could I have done better on this rotation and
what do I need to do better in the future to be a great
doctor? And If you start telling me how good I am,
I will get up and walk out.

It was important to me to get better and the only way to do that
was to fully embrace my failures and weak spots. And as to saying I
didn't want praise, I just wanted them to know that I already knew
what I did well—I needed to know how to get better.

That habit is one I have seen in every great leader and elite athlete
I have ever met. To be sure, obsessively focusing on failure can be unhealthy, but no less unhealthy than an excessively optimistic view,
paving over failures with the patina of success. Failure is not only a

part of life, it's an essential part of leading, especially leading innovative teams. That is why Nelson Mandela said, "Do not judge me by my
successes. Judge me by how many times I fell down and got up again."[2]

For many people, being the leader is synonymous with success,
connoting as it does, the victories and not the defeats that led them
there. My late friend Coach John Madden is famous for his many say-
ings, including this one:

Winning is a great deodorant.[3]

Success is indeed a great deodorant—but it is always born from
failure. It is curious that success is rarely as interesting as failure—
and is not nearly as educating. My father, affectionately known in our
family as Grandpa Jim, said to me, after some real or perceived bump
in the road I suffered, "Son, there's a reason there's a Book of Job in
the Bible." Wise words . . .

FAILURE IS NOT THE OPPOSITE OF SUCCESS—IT IS A PART OF SUCCESS

The thousands of NFL players I have known over the years all remember the mistakes, the busted plays, the missed tackles, the dropped
passes, the interceptions, and the missed field goals much more than
they remember the great plays they got right. They rose to—and stayed
at—the high level they occupy as NFL players by relentlessly considering not just what they did well, but how they could have done even
better. Leading requires the same mentality, savoring success—but
analyzing failure out of a consuming desire to improve.

FAILURE MOTIVATES

Tom Brady, seven-time Super Bowl winner, five-time Super Bowl
MVP, and five-time NFL MVP, who was selected by the New England
Patriots as the 199th pick in Round 6 of the 2000 NFL Draft, can not
only remember, but name every quarterback who was taken before
him, in which round, and by which team. He didn't celebrate being
drafted—he used where he was drafted to motivate himself.[4]

Was Tom's draft status a liability . . . or an asset? You know the answer—it's all in the point of view—the attitude vs. the aptitude.

Two of the greatest NCAA basketball coaches of all time are John Wooden of UCLA (who won 10 NCAA championships, including 7 in a row) and Mike Krzyzewski (Coach K) of Duke, who won 5 NCAA championships and amassed 1,202 victories, the most of any Division I coach. I had the chance to interview nearly 50 players who these two great men coached, as well as Coach K himself.[5] Most people would assume that these men repeatedly told their players, "Win!" But the fact is, everyone to whom I spoke said neither of these men *ever* said that . . . What they did say was to pay attention to details, to visualize playing well, and to execute the fundamentals incessantly. But "Win!" was never said—and yet they won . . .

The same is true of innovation—while we aspire to "Success!," failure is always a distinct possibility. There is no such thing as a "perfect game," except in baseball. (And baseball is a game in which failing two out of every three times at bat over a career earns you a ticket to Cooperstown.)

Failure is not the *opposite* of success—failure
is a *part* of success.

Use failure to find ways to improve and use the hard stone of failure to sharpen the instruments that will surgically guide your successes. Failure should be our teacher, not our pallbearer. And "a failure" isn't "a loser." A failure is an innovation that isn't completely successful (and none ever are). A loser is someone who doesn't learn from failure.

Embrace failure . . . but don't be a loser.

It is not failure that paralyzes us—it is the fear of failure. Mark Twain supposedly said:

*I have known a great many troubles in my life, but most of
them never happened.*[6]

Sometimes we suffer more slights in our fearful minds than reality ever gives us. Diogenes was asked what his favorite wine was, to which he said, "Someone else's." The same is true of failure—we love other people's failures—as if they immunize us against our own.

Don't let your failures define you; don't let failure become your jailer, locking you in and keeping the key. You have the key—never relinquish it; many people do involuntarily.

The ancient wisdom of Kohelet or Ecclesiastes pertains as well:

> *The race is not to the swift or the battle to the strong, nor does food come to the wise or wealth to the brilliant or favor to the learned; but time and chance happen to them all.*[7]

There is no better lesson in leading than to accept that time, chance, and failure—as well as success—happen to us all. So, embrace failure and develop your *"failure muscles"* in your quest—not for perfection—but for *your* best version of excellence.

DEVELOPING YOUR FAILURE MUSCLES

> *Personally, I am always ready to learn—*
> *but I do not always wish to be taught.*
> WINSTON S. CHURCHILL[8]

There are countless books and speeches celebrating "How I did it . . ." Good for them and for their success, which I am sure they richly deserve. But we need to develop our "failure muscles." Here are my thoughts on what they are and how to employ them.

I. MAKE FAILURE YOUR FUEL

Abby Wambach, like Mia Hamm, is also one of the most legendary soccer players of all time, who played on the US Women's National Team (USWNT) from 2003 to 2015. She is first in all-time goals scored for the USWNT and second in World Cup history, holding first place until 2013. Her teams won World Cups, NCAA National Championships, and Olympic Gold Medals. Her reputation for ferocity, tenacity, and perseverance remains to all those who know the sport.

But she has also been fierce and tenacious in her demands for women's and minority rights, both during her playing career and after. In 2016, she was awarded ESPN's first Icon Award, along with Kobe Bryant and Peyton Manning, as legendary icons in their respective sports. But as she walked off the stage, she was seized by the thought that, unlike Peyton and Kobe, she was not walking off into a future of financial success, despite her achievements, and set about to fight for equal pay for women soccer players.

On May 16, 2018, she stepped to the stage at Radio City Music Hall to deliver the commencement address for Barnard College. The speech was a viral phenomenon and has been viewed millions of times and spawned her best-selling book *Wolfpack: How to Come Together, Unleash Our Power, and Change the Game*,[9] which was the theme of the talk. It was based on the story of the wolf reintroduction program in Yellowstone National Park and how the wolves literally changed the entire biology of the park and altered the flow of the rivers. (Full disclosure, my wife Maureen was the executive producer of *Druid Peak,* an award-winning fictional account of the same theme with a coming-of-age story as the background.)

In the speech, Abby presents four rules, the first and most important of which is:

Make failure your fuel!

She emphasizes that failure is fuel, fuel is power, and all of us must use our failures to "power up!"

Great advice from one of the greatest soccer players in history . . . and great advice for us.

I had the honor of sharing the dais with Abby at a national meeting, where her tenacity and ferocity—as well as her innate kindness—came through with every sentence. And my picture of her holding a copy of Maureen's award-winning movie, *Druid Peak,* fills a treasured spot in our home.

There are many tools to study both failures and successes—learn them and use them. In theology and literature, it is known as exegesis, which is the process of unpacking and analyzing things by doing a critical interpretation. Kevin, our middle son, was a Marine infantry officer, and he taught me the importance of after action reviews (AARs), in which the combat team asks a series of questions after a mission, all designed to improve the next mission. In sports, it's film study. In medicine it is a morbidity, mortality, *and improvement* (MMI) conference designed to say "What happened?" "What could have gone better?" and "How can we improve the next time?" My NFL players spend three to five times as much time in the film room analyzing their actions than they do either in practice or in games. Regardless of whether you succeeded or failed, develop the habits of *looking backward* with honesty, transparency, and an open heart—so you can *look forward* more astutely.

2. EMBRACE AND ACCEPT BOTH SUCCESSES AND FAILURES

Both are inevitable and both must be valued for what they bring. As Kipling wrote in "If":

> *If you can meet with Triumph and Disaster*
> *And treat those two imposters just the same . . .*[10]

Don't be surprised by success *or* failure and learn from both. Coach Kara Lawson of Duke Women's Basketball and a Hall of Fame player tells her players:

> *Don't play to prove the people who <u>don't</u> believe in you <u>wrong</u>,*
> *play to prove the people who <u>do</u> believe in you <u>right</u>.*[11]

Lead innovation to prove the people who believe in you are right.

3. RECOGNIZE THE TOXICITY OF "IF ONLY . . ." AND "BUT . . ."

When failures occur, find a way to immunize yourself against two of the most toxic words on the planet: "If only . . ." and "But . . ." You know the drill—we all do—when failure (or partial success) occurs, we say "If only . . ."

- "I had been bigger, stronger, swifter, smarter, etc."
- "I had studied harder or done the right things or at the right time."
- "I hadn't gotten married when I did."
- "I didn't have kids when I did."
- "I had taken out a fixed-rate mortgage instead of an ARM."

"But . . ." is "If only's" equally venomous cousin, as in, "Yes I failed, but . . ."

- "So did you."
- "I tried really hard."
- "It wasn't fair."
- "COVID happened."
- "Who knew the market would fall."

These ideas ricochet around your brain like bullets, leaving horrific damage in their wake. Excise them from your vocabulary and exorcise them from your mind. Here's an example of someone who did just that . . .

THE TERRIBLE TOLL OF "IF ONLY . . ."

In small-town Louisiana in the 1950s, ambitions were easy, but fulfilling dreams was harder. A tall, skinny kid started his high school years as a clarinetist in the band but was asked to try out for football as a sophomore. Unfortunately, he quickly tore his Achilles tendon, requiring surgery and ending his season. Many people would have said, "If only . . . I hadn't torn my Achilles tendon I could have been a football player." He was back as a junior, but he developed osteomyelitis, ending that season.

Again, he might have said, "If only . . ." He didn't, coming back as a senior for another shot, but . . . had a severe hip injury.

Fortunately, he was a great track athlete and won the state championship in the hurdles, which earned him a partial scholarship to Northwestern Louisiana State College. But they told him that if he would agree to be on the football team, he would get a full scholarship, even if he didn't play. (As the formerly skinny kid told me, "That's how desperate they were to field a team!")

He could have said, "If only . . ." or "But I've had too many injuries to play football." But he didn't.

Four years later, that skinny kid had filled out and persevered in football and track and was drafted in the 10th round of the NFL draft, where he played 16 years as a tight end for the St. Louis Cardinals and Dallas Cowboys. In 1994, Jackie Smith was inducted into the Pro Football Hall of Fame, an honor only 371 men have attained, out of the 6 billion men who have lived on the planet . . . because he never said, "If only . . ." or "But . . ."[12]

Jackie Smith is both a friend and mentor, from whom I continue to learn. (And if you haven't heard Jackie sing the "Star Spangled Banner," you haven't lived . . .)

4. THE ELIXIR OF LAUGHTER AND RECOVERY

Since failure is inevitable—particularly when innovating, don't just embrace and accept it—find ways to laugh about it so you and your team can recover. In every film room in every sport in every country, as you "break the film down," there will be plays in which you did so terribly it is cringeworthy—and your teammates will laugh. So should you. There's a reason ESPN's *SportsCenter* has a "Not Top 10" list every week. Treat laughter and recovery as the elixir it is.

5. DEVELOP YOUR "FORGIVE AND FORGET" SKILLS

Don't get too bogged down in the doldrums of festering resentment. As Nelson Mandela said,

> *Resentment is like drinking poison and then hoping*
> *it will kill your enemies.*[13]

Don't let resentment be the poison you drink—or the water in which you bathe. Make it an elixir for learning.

And the first person you must forgive is *you*, because if you can't forgive yourself, you can never forgive others—and you *must* forgive others. "Hold the mirror up to the B Team members" to show them how their behavior affects others. But don't stare in the mirror, focusing excessively on your faults. People with depression sometimes look in the mirror with self-loathing. As I told a friend of mine who struggles with depression, "You would *never* treat another person the harsh way you treat yourself. You're one of the kindest people I know—except to yourself." Forgive and forget your perceived frailties, faults, failures, and vulnerabilities. (See below.)

TIME TO PUT HER DOWN

We tried to expose our boys to great traditions from many religious viewpoints. This story resonated with us . . . and the boys. In Zen tradition, the story is told of the Zen master and his acolyte, who were traveling together as they walked from one village to the next. They came upon a huge pool of water, which completely covered the road on which they were traveling, which meant they had to wade through it. As they began to remove their sandals and roll up their pants, a dowager came upon them and quickly began to berate them, saying, "You filthy beggars—pick me up on your shoulders immediately and carry me across this muddy pool! Do it quickly!" The master lifted her on his shoulders and began the struggle of carrying her across. But she continued her harassment, saying, "Hurry up! Hurry up! What's wrong with you? Why are you taking so long?"

Putting her down safely on the dry road past the pool, the master straightened and faced the lady, who continued the barrage, "You filthy dog, how dare you look at me? Turn around and face away from me!"

They resumed their journey. For the next five miles, the acolyte wondered aloud in amazement, "How could that terrible person do that to you? Why didn't you say anything back to her?" After five miles, the Zen master smiled at his acolyte and said, "I put her down five miles ago. Don't you think it's time for *you* to put her down?"

It's usually wise to put our failures down quickly after they occur, learning what we can from them. Don't keep carrying them down the road.

6. TAKE A PAGE . . . OR TWO . . . OR TWENTY FROM BRENÉ BROWN—DON'T JUST ACCEPT VULNERABILITY . . . EMBRACE IT!

Sometimes the simplest of messages can have the most profound effect. You may know the story of Brené Brown, who in 2012 gave a TEDx Houston talk that she assumed would have little or no impact . . . and that has now been viewed 66 million times! Brené spoke movingly about how shame and its sister—vulnerability—are critical for growth and making failure your fuel. They are not the same thing. Shame is a focus on self, and taken too seriously leads to fear of disconnection, while excruciating vulnerability arises out of a focus on behaviors—actions as we lead in the active voice. Vulnerability should allow us to be seen, to be *really* seen, and not as we hope to be, but as who we are. We need the courage to be imperfect, even as we seek improvement, which leads to compassion for ourselves and others and the connection through authenticity to living wholeheartedly. Focusing on shame, however, leads to two demonic destinations: "Never Good Enough" and "Who Do You Think You Are?"—whose close relative is of course, "Imposter Syndrome."[14] If you haven't followed Brené's work . . . start now! (brenebrown.com).

7. DESPAIR COMES TO ALL OF US—IT STAYS WITH A FEW

Don't let despair stay with you, rent free in your head. When it visits, and it will, greet it—and then throw it out. Deal with the inevitable negativity and failure in life—then put them down, learn from them, and use them to anticipate better in the future.

8. TRANSLATE EXPERIENCE TO ACTIONS—HUDDLE UP

Use these tools to develop a new game plan, since *better informed* means *better executed*. Make the game plan a team effort, jointly developed, because "If they aren't with you on the takeoff, they won't be with you on the landing." Before each play football players "Huddle Up" to assure everyone knows the next play, their assignments, and how they seamlessly fit together. Huddles get everyone on the same page with shared mental models. Use huddles in your business and your life to pull the team together.

9. CALLING AN AUDIBLE

Every quarterback in the NFL learns to call audibles, changing the play at the line of scrimmage, when they see their opponent is in a different formation than expected. (Each quarterback does it differently, from Tom Brady pointing at his helmet and shouting "Alert, Alert" to Peyton Manning's iconic "Omaha" call.) Calling an audible simply changes the *play*, not the *game plan*. Failure happens when our expectations are confronted with a different reality than we expected, but audibles aren't called to abort failure before it happens.

10. CREATIVE ENERGY

Joan Kyes was a wise psychiatric nurse with whom I co-taught frequently. She taught me about the concept of "Creative Energy."[15] We've all known people in our lives who seem to have inexhaustible wells of energy, bouncing from project to project like the Energizer Bunny. But others seem to be constantly and perpetually exhausted—completely drained of energy.

Joan taught me that every person has basically the same size "energy reservoir," as she called it. When you undertake a project, you open an "energy packet" from that reservoir and use it for the project. The size of the energy packet depends upon the size of the project and the energy needed to complete it. "Mowing the lawn" requires a smaller energy packet than "remodeling the house" or "finding a new job." (For me, "taking out the trash" is a massive energy packet, while "writing an article" is not . . .)

But here's the great insight—you don't get the energy back until you finish the task and make an "energy deposit" into the reservoir. The key to having high, functional energy is to "close your packets!" I found that insight simple, incisive—and absolutely brilliant. Feel exhausted? You have too many energy packets open. Close some of your packets and redeposit them. Feeling energetic? Open a packet and start the next project on your list.

II. 3 GOOD THINGS

The field of positive psychology turns from a focus on the negative, pathological things in life to those things that are going well, building on them for the present—and the future. One of the simplest but most powerful concepts is called *3 Good Things.*[16] 3 Good Things asks people to pause, reflect, and reconsider at the end of the day and write down 3 Good Things that happened that day, as well as their role in making them happen. When compared with pharmacological treatments in patients with depression, 3 Good Things was both more effective and more lasting in its effects.

Develop the habit of 3 Good Things for yourself, your team, and your family. It will help you forgive yourself and others, and end the day on a positive note. Which means starting the next day well . . . (the 3goodthings.org/about).

THE HEALING POWER OF FAILURE

One of the greatest lessons arising from my career in trauma is gleaning a deep understanding of the majestic power of the healing process at a cellular and biochemical level. Trauma, injury, wounds— all connote a profoundly negative experience that no one desires. And yet it is through that inexorable process that we become stronger. Injury is inevitable . . . but healing is invaluable.

The balletic cascade of healing requires minute coordination of multiple different cell types performing different, yet highly related functions. Quickly after tissue injury, a fibrin clot forms, serving as a dam, an obstruction to flow, which not only stops the hemorrhage, but attracts cellular allies and leads to angiogenesis—the development of new and fresh blood vessels. The fibrin clot is paradoxical, obstructing flow on the short term, while signaling the cavalry to come to the healing process. I'm no dancer—ask my wife—but it's impossible to study trauma and healing without seeing the beautiful dance of the multiple cells, eliciting their biochemical signals of interleukins, pro-inflammatory markers, leukotrienes, and many others, like musical notes, all of which come together to form the symphony of healing. As the fibroblasts are summoned to do their work and angiogenesis begins, the wound becomes progressively stronger until bonds have formed and healing has been completed. The scar remodels over time, retracting down and losing its angry red appearance. And the scar should simply serve as a reminder of the regenerative power of the process . . .[17]

TAKING ADVERSITY TO THE FINAL FOUR

In March 2006 the Duke Men's lacrosse team was stacked with talent, rated #1 in the country and expected to compete for a national championship, which Duke had never won. Following a lacrosse party the night before, three of the lacrosse players were accused of rape, although it was patently apparent no such thing had ever happened. Fueled by lies from an ambitious prosecutor and his equally nefarious detectives with the local police department, the Duke Lacrosse Hoax was born. A group of 88 Duke faculty, self-righteously calling themselves "The Gang of 88," made a "Wanted" poster with the pictures of all the lacrosse players and festooned it across the campus, the town, and, via news outlets, the world. Full disclosure, one of those players on the team was our son Kevin, who was not accused (later a decorated Marine infantry officer with two highly kinetic tours in Afghanistan) and Maureen and I were the co-chairs of the Duke lacrosse parents group—The Devils' Advocates.

Despite no evidence to support the hoax, it took over a year for North Carolina Attorney General Roy Cooper to dismiss and disbar the prosecutor that filed the charges and proclaim that all Duke lacrosse players were "INNOCENT." (The discovery of the DNA evidence conclusively proving their innocence began with my review of the evidence and was masterfully presented by Brad Bannon, a highly skilled attorney.)

But the trauma caused to the team, the Duke community, and even the nation was significant. Indeed, it wasn't clear that there would even be a Duke lacrosse team until Maureen and I testified to the committee chaired by the eminent Duke law professor, James Coleman, summarizing the evidence compiled by all the lacrosse parents that supported these young men's character and accomplishments.

Since the coach had been fired at the outset of the hoax and with a mass hysteria to assume the guilt of the players, a new coach had to be recruited. In May 2006, on the way to the airport to give a speech, I made a phone call to Coach John Danowski, then the head coach at Hofstra and whose son Matt was a pivotal part of Duke's success, imploring him to consider taking the job. After a search committee unanimously agreed, "Coach Dino" as he is affectionately known, became the Duke Men's Lacrosse coach.

But among his remarks after being selected, he said, "I chose to accept the challenge at Duke because I wanted to make a difference in these young men's lives. But in fact, they have already made a difference in mine." Coach focused not on the X's and O's of coaching, but instead relied on his background as a coach with his master's degree in . . . counseling. He focused on healing, not winning, so that the traumas they had experienced would not scar them for the rest of their lives. And when, on Memorial Day weekend, Duke played in the national championship game, he told the team:

Guys, you think this is the biggest day of your lives. Gentlemen, this isn't even *close* to the biggest day of your lives. The day you graduate, that's a bigger day. The day you get your first job, that's a bigger day. The day you get married, that's a *much* bigger day, as are the days your children are born. Now just go out there and have fun!

While Duke lost that game 12–11, every player on that team had fun. And they will never forget Coach Dino's speech, including our son Kevin.[18]

Even during crisis, healing has a power well worth investing in as you lead. And while they did not win that game, Coach Dino has since won three NCAA titles at Duke . . . but has healed countless young men, which is far more significant.

LIMITS BEGIN WHERE VISION ENDS

It's always impossible until it gets done.

NELSON MANDELA[19]

When in my junior year I decided to take the required courses to apply to medical school, I was told more than once that it simply wasn't possible to fit them in, much less to do so while playing football and majoring in theology. I thought of something from history about the impossible becoming possible.

LIMITS BEGIN WHERE VISION ENDS

On May 6, 1954, something happened, which to the best of anyone's knowledge had never been done before in the history of mankind. During my talks, I ask the audience to hazard their best guess as to what it was. "Telstar," "Sputnik," "first manned space flight," and more recently "invention of the internet" are common answers.

On that day, Roger Bannister, then a medical student at Oxford University, ran the world's first sub-four-minute mile at Iffley Road Track in Oxford, England, in 3:59.4. The feat staggered the world, not the least of which was because not only that it had never been done, it was thought by the best scientific minds of the time to be impossible. In fact, three of the leading medical journals published articles stating emphatically that doing so would not only be impossible but . . . fatal, including mechanisms by which the death would ensue. And yet Bannister did it—how?

Bannister—and his fellow runners and medical students Chris Chataway and Chris Brasher—had a vision for precisely how it could be done. Their vision did not focus exclusively on speed, but on developing oxygen consumption, measured as VO_2Max. Using VO_2Max measurements in the lab on treadmills, they were able to show that it was not strength or speed alone that was necessary, but the ability to most efficiently use oxygen to drive the engine. After perfecting their training, on May 6, 1954, they set out to prove their theory, with Brasher and Chataway pacing Bannister through the four laps. Despite being told the feat was impossible—and likely fatal—Bannister ran a mile in 3 minutes, 59.4 seconds. Limits disappeared because he had the vision to achieve it.

The impossible became possible because they had a vision for how it could be done. But consider this: Never in the history of mankind had it ever been done, but . . .

How long was it until 10 men had done it?

The answer is stunning—two years and three months after the impossible was made possible by the vision to do it, 10 men had done it. In fact, one year and two weeks after May 6, 1954, three men ran a sub-four-minute mile in the same day—in the same race! Something that had previously been thought not only impossible, but physiologically unattainable has now become almost commonplace, since by 2012, 1,000 men had done it and last year the 2,000th person accomplished it.[20]

The power of informed and educated vision to make the impossible—and possibly fatal—both possible and commonplace is undeniable. Isn't that precisely what Nelson Mandela and his African National Congress colleagues did in ending apartheid in South Africa? Isn't that what the Mercury, Apollo, Gemini, and Space Shuttle astronauts did? The examples are countless and everywhere, and not just on the world stage, but in everyday life. Every single mother does the impossible in raising her family, every child from an underprivileged background does the impossible when they go to college to realize their dream, every patient who fights through heart disease, diabetes, or cancer does the impossible as they fight their battle.

Because of their vision, they have no limits . . .

The same is true of Edison, whose vision that electricity could be turned into light was undeterred by the 1,000 failures of how *not* to do it. And whenever the inevitable critics voice their negative opinions, I always remember this story.

In the early 1990s two young entrepreneurs who had met while camp counselors transformed the banking industry by facing a statistical lens to analyze credit cards, which, while the most profitable part of the banking business, were almost totally ignored. They developed a statistical method to identify risk groups in the credit card industry, where customers were rated according to their creditworthiness by grades from A to F. The financial industry at the time pursued "A" rated customers since they presented a low risk of not paying their credit cards off eventually. Throughout the industry, the "A" group was considered a uniform group of similar low credit default risk. But the two entrepreneurs, Rich and Nigel, developed the information-based strategy (IBS), a statistical means to show that the A-rated category actually comprised 100 different levels of credit card risk. They further developed the concept that those 100 categories could be stratified into what they termed "Love 'Ems" and "Kill Ya's." Kill Ya's were a statistically distinct group of A-rated credit risks who not only paid their bills, but did so promptly, meaning the bank issuing the card received no interest accrued and therefore were not profitable as customers. Love 'Em's also eventually paid their card balances, but did so by paying the "minimum payment due," meaning that they paid 18–26 percent annual interest on the balances, which were carried over to the next month—hence increasing profits dramatically for the banks. Rich and Nigel saw differentiation where others saw uniformity—they saw innovation where others saw accepted, established doctrine. They saw the power of IBS to deliver mass customization, now recognized as one of the most powerful forces in business.

They pitched this concept to 26 banks—each of which sent them packing, often shaking their heads and wondering just what these two guys were thinking with this radical departure from banking norms. (One bank president threatened to throw Rich out the window.) But the 27th bank, Signet Bank in Richmond, Virginia, decided to give these fellows a shot with a trial of the process.

Rich and Nigel did pretty well, since they eventually spun off from Signet and formed a financial company of their own, which did reasonably well in the credit card business. I think I forgot to mention that the company they founded is . . . Capital One, one of the largest financial institutions in the world. "Rich" is Rich Fairbank, CEO of Capital One, and "Nigel" is Nigel Morris, then president and COO.[21]

Success is worthless . . . but failure is priceless, as Rich and Nigel and their team proved.

Rich is a close friend, as is Nigel, and Nigel, for full disclosure, was an investor in one of my entrepreneurial ventures. They both told me that the 26 failures honed their ideas and their presentation of the IBS. But those failures also constantly annealed their commitment to their Deep Joy—completely transforming the financial industry through deep exegesis of information. Rich famously said, "Credit cards aren't banking—they're information." And Nigel describes himself as a "raging empiricist," fanatically committed to using data to transform leading. Visionaries are often deeply committed to their innovations, seeing as they do something others haven't—or can't. Years after Capital One's founding, I had dinner with Rich and we were discussing obsessive-compulsive disorder, or OCD. I said, "Rich, I've learned that just because it's 'OC' doesn't necessarily means it's a 'D.'" Rich laughed uproariously and told his wife Chris the insight, who said, "You got that right when it comes to Rich!"

But if people don't share the vision of the visionary . . . they may think they are hallucinating.

TAKE OURSELVES LIGHTLY

The great writer G. K. Chesterton was once asked by a child how angels could fly. He answered simply, "Angels can fly because they take themselves lightly." [22] That's good advice for all of us in these turbulent, often contentious times. As we consider the calculus between our failures and our successes, we could do worse than treating ourselves lightly.

With that understanding of the value of failure, we turn to why "The C-suite is worthless . . . but the We-suite is priceless."

MAKING FAILURE YOUR FUEL SUMMARY

- Failure is not the opposite of success—it is an essential part of success.
- Make failure your fuel.
- Develop your "Failure Muscles."
- Take yourself and others lightly.

5

THE C-SUITE AND
THE WE-SUITE

It's not what I <u>say</u> that matters.
It's what they <u>do</u> on the court that matters.

—COACH MIKE KRZYZEWSKI[1]

I attended medical school at one of the most prestigious institutions in the world—Duke University School of Medicine. Medical schools typically have a hierarchical structure, with the deans and professors at the top. "From the professors on down" was a common refrain in medical school's ivory towers, and the furthest down the hierarchy were the lowly medical students—*us*. And no academic department in the school embraced this belief more than the departments of surgery, where authority was the dominant ethos.

But the chair of the Duke Department of Surgery was David C. Sabiston, MD, one of the most venerated surgeons in the world. He was internationally renowned—not just for his legendary surgical skill, but also for being the editor-in-chief of the *Sabiston Textbook of Surgery*, which every medical student across many generations owned.

Dr. Sabiston had a unique approach to medical students. On the first day of the surgical rotation, he met with all the medical students to welcome them to the rotation. He had not only memorized all our names and faces, but also knew a great deal about our backgrounds.

For example, on the first day of our rotation, he said to me, "Thom, the disciplines you will learn in surgery must be similar to the disciplines of theology and football—I want your thoughts on that at the end of your rotation."

To Traci Rouault, one of my classmates, he smiled as he said, "Traci, given the fact that your grandfather was the famous painter Georges Rouault, I trust that your inherited artistic talents will translate to surgery as well."

He told all the students—with the chief residents in the room as witnesses—"The Duke Department of Surgery believes in the critical importance of education—from the medical students on *down*." He flipped the script by daring to put the medical students at the top of the hierarchy, not the bottom. As grueling as the hours on the surgical rotation were, it was a favorite for all medical students since we knew we were at the top.

Similarly, the We-suite should be at the top of your organization, not the potentates in the C-suite. The C-suite should be fanatically dedicated first to those they serve—whether patients, clients, customers, or family members—but second to those who do the work, the We-suite. This is the essence of servant leading, which we'll discuss in more detail in the next chapter. It's not what *you say*, but what *they do* that matters.

Since the way we're working . . . isn't working, we turn to a critical question: Who are the best architects of our future successes, born out of our current failures?

For decades, the people in the C-suite—the potentates, The Bosses, or in families, the parents—have been granted the authority to set the strategic direction of organizations, charting their course and guiding the way.

It is time for a radical revision of that paradigm.

Because . . .

The C-suite has a completely different function
than the We-suite.
We've just gotten the C-suite's role wrong.

The C-suite is worthless in its current role . . . but it can be priceless in its new role. It's not that we have expected *too much* of the
C-suite, it's that we have expected the *wrong things* of the C-suite.

And it's not that we have expected *too little* of the We-suite, it's
that we haven't expected *enough*—to tap into its enormous power, creativity, and energy.

Let's take the next step in our journey with some definitions.

THE C-SUITE VS. THE WE-SUITE

Through a combination of hard work, tenacity, intelligence—and occasionally, luck—people in the C-suite have risen over many years to
a place of supervision, oversight, and, well . . . power. But, properly
considered, they have a different role than we have supposed. And a
key consideration is that the new role for the C-suite is much more
satisfying and gratifying than the stratospheric, but often sterile
space they now occupy. Frankly, the way we're working . . . isn't working for the C-suite, either.

The hidden, dormant source of energy, creativity, and innovation
of an organization or team resides in the We-suite, the collective
force of those who do the work and uniquely understand the staggering potential of how the *work could be done.* Organizations and families alike have neglected to recognize the transformational energy
unleashed from the We-suite and encouraged by the C-suite.

Who's the C-suite? Bosses, potentates, heads, coaches, parents.

Who's the We-suite? Team, peons, hands, players, children.

The Bosses are often called the *heads* of departments, divisions,
or the family, while the team is the *hands*, as in the hands in the fields,
with its obvious if unintended plantation-mentality connotation.

People often tell me, "It must be nice to be your own Boss!" and I
have to laugh when I hear it. In reality, I have 2,500 bosses—each one

of the players in the National Football League—we are a union of players, not staff. Add in their wives and significant others, their kids, and their parents, and as I say, "I'm the only doctor I know who has 10,000 patients." If you have 10,000 patients, you have 10,000 bosses. Far more important and to the point is this fundamental insight:

> *Everyone* is their own boss—most people just don't realize it.
> Some people don't want to accept that responsibility.
> Being a leader means admitting The Boss doesn't
> have what you want.
> But *you* do . . .

I reiterate a point made in Chapter 1—don't *aspire* to be a leader, you *already are* a leader. You are your own boss, motivator, and the ultimate arbiter of your success and the success of your team. This isn't some self-help adage—it is born out of long experience in many settings.

The C-suite does have a different function than has traditionally been assumed. We have assumed that those who reside there have all the answers, and from those answers they will show *us* the way toward the future. As Dr. Phil might say, "How's that working for you?"

The C-suite's actual role is not to innovate, but to act as stewards to help the We-suite innovate by coaching and mentoring the team, not ordering them once more unto the breach. So, the question is, "Who is responsible for implementing new systems and processes through innovation in a culture of trust?"

THE ANSWER TO "WHO?" IS "YOU!"

Who is going to change the systems and processes of your life, at work and at home?

> "Who" is "you!"

Most companies and the teams comprising them believe that it is the job of the C-suite—The Bosses—to drive change and innovation. They think that it is their exclusive province, right, and privilege to do so. Nothing could be further from the truth. For too long we have entrusted and genuflected to the power of the throne instead of the power of the people doing the work.

Do you want The Boss, the C-suite, to author the new way of doing things? I have been a member of countless C-suites in my own career, and I can tell you with confidence that if you leave it up to us to devise a new system . . .

We will screw it up!

That's not because we are trying to send the team in the wrong direction . . . it's because we don't *do the work* and therefore *don't understand the work* sufficiently to recommend precise, surgical changes. We can only anticipate and chart out the general direction. If you rely on the C-suite for answers to "The way we're working . . . isn't working," you will get top-down, underinformed (or worse, misinformed) solutions, not the requisite bottoms-up approach to innovation.

People who consider themselves The Boss (and have spent substantial parts of their lives laboring to get there) consider themselves the most important person in the room.

People who consider themselves leaders know that Job #1 is to make everyone else in the room feel that *they* are the most important person—because they are![2]

THE WE-SUITE OF THE US WOMEN'S SOCCER TEAM

We met Mia Hamm and Abby Wambach in the two previous chapters, each of whom were legendary members of the US Women's National Team (USWNT), winners of multiple championships in international competition. We also learned of Abby's fierce commitment to the concept of equal pay for equal work. Both the men's and women's teams work for the US Soccer Federation (USSF), with which they have collective bargaining agreements (CBAs), just as my players in the NFL do.

In 2016, the USWNT filed suit against USSF for violations of the Equal Pay Act and Title VII of the Civil Rights Act of 1964, since the women's team members were paid 38 percent of what the men's team was paid at that time. The legal challenge was led by Jeffrey Kessler of Winston & Strawn, who, for full disclosure, also represents the NFLPA in our negotiations with the NFL.

Despite numerous legal setbacks, including summary judgements against the women, in 2022, a settlement was reached with the US Soccer Federation and the USWNT not only assuring equal pay on a go-forward and ongoing basis, but paying $22 million for past discrimination and $2 million for a fund to benefit USWNT members in pursuing their post-career goals.

The tenacity and ferocity of the players themselves—the We-Suite—was both the genesis of the suit and the fuel that kept the flame alive. There is no substitute for the voice of the player-patient—an outcome that is expected to affect gender pay not only in sports but across society.

THE FRICTION OF CHANGE

In its research, change management firm Prosci found that people in different positions in an organization resist change at different levels—getting progressively more resistant toward the middle. While only 9 percent of executives and directors, and 16 percent of senior-level managers resist change, 42 percent of mid-level managers are resistant to change. On the other hand, just 27 percent of frontline employees resist change, with "Other" making up the remaining 6 percent of the total.[3]

According to Prosci's research, the end result of this resistance to change includes such things as: lack in participation in the change, openly expressing negative emotions about the change—complaining, anger, bad attitudes, and so on—absenteeism, reverting to old ways, and decreased productivity.[4]

Ultimately, most people don't mind *change*—they mind *being changed*.

Several points deserve emphasis:

- Without resistance, there is no change, so welcome resistance.
- Resistance = Uncertainty

- Staunch resistance = Deep uncertainty
- Leading requires the skills of change acceleration, including anticipating and even encouraging resistance.
- Resistance in physics is *friction*, an appropriate metaphor for change.
- Innovative change = Resistance = Uncertainty = Friction

How do we lead while effectively dealing with friction? We cannot live in a frictionless world because change is certain. Relying on the We-suite reduces the friction of change and is an antidote for anxiety and uncertainty, lubricating the development of better systems and processes. Further, the culture we create by leading in the active voice is the oil lubricating innovation in as frictionless an environment as possible.

Because of my work at the Pentagon on 9/11, and subsequently serving on three Defense Science Board task forces advising the secretary of defense, I had the opportunity to spend several days on nuclear aircraft carriers, observing naval and Marine aviation operations.

Today's Nimitz-class aircraft carriers are crewed by more than 6,000 men and women, whose interactions to maintain, taxi, launch, and land the many aircraft of all types—from fighters to submarine chasers to helicopters and more—needed to support the ship's mission is a remarkably beautiful ballet of movement. [5]

Watching the yellow-vested "shooters" and their teammates—each with different-colored vests or shirts, depending on their job—launch these magnificent aircraft off a pitching carrier deck using a remarkably powerful catapult, and then retrieving them afterward, is a stunning experience. I remarked to Admiral Denby Starling, in charge of the USS George Washington CVN-73 carrier fleet and a naval aviator himself, how much this process reminded me of my NFL players working together, each with a different set of skills to attain victory.

He smiled, saying, "If they're not with you on the takeoff, they won't be with you on the landing."[6]

The same is true of all our teams and organizations. Make sure they are with you on the takeoff so they can be with you on the landing.

If you are in the C-suite, be sure the We-suite is with you on the takeoff.

If you are in the We-suite, demand that you be there on the takeoff.

COURAGE OVER FRICTION

During my career with the NFLPA, I have worked with three executive directors and six presidents, the latter of which is a player or immediately retired former player elected by the Board of Player Representatives.

JC Tretter, our current president, played nine years in the NFL as a center for the Green Bay Packers and the Cleveland Browns. He is a Cornell-educated man who is as articulate, intelligent, and . . . courageous as anyone with whom I have ever worked, inside or outside football. His ferocity on the field carries over to his duties as our president. My NFL players, without exception, have courage on the football field that is exceeded only by their courage in the boardroom. JC embodies that better than anyone.

JC knew from our briefings that the clear data from over ten years comparing lower extremity (LEX) injuries in the league between grass fields and artificial-turf fields showed a higher injury rate on artificial turf. However, in 2021, that gap closed briefly, causing the NFL's bigwigs to crow that there was now no difference between the field surfaces. But the data from 2022 blew that argument apart, showing a return to the ten-year trend. The league's spokesman nonetheless continued to misrepresent the data, saying there was no difference.

In late April 2023, JC wrote in his column to the players (which is widely disseminated across the internet and multiple websites), a brilliant and detailed critique of the data, showing clearly and conclusively that grass fields resulted in fewer LEX injuries—without question.[7]

Did JC's column cause friction with the NFL? You bet it did—they issued an immediate screed crying foul. Just one problem: the NFL had neither the science nor the data upon which they could argue against JC's well-reasoned and factually supported argument. Did it take courage for JC to take on the most powerful sports league in the world? You bet it did. But he would be the first person to tell you it was more than worth it.

Courage and science win over power every time, particularly when the We-suite (the players union) represents the viewpoint of those doing the work.

A FALSE DICHOTOMY

When we empower the We-suites in our organizations, we allow them to use the tools of leading to envision a better way of doing things. Once the new vision is enacted, the We-suite returns to their management skills, keeping the new systems and processes (the *smart stuff*) working aligned with the new vision.

However, the C-suite versus the We-suite concept is a false dichotomy. It is not an either/or situation, but a both/and. When properly considered and empowered, We-suites evolve as needed to execute innovative change in an environment of trust for the specific problems they face, using their unique knowledge of the challenge. The We-suite doesn't usurp the function of the C-suite, but its members do embrace the challenges of innovation.

So explains the great management thinker, Ken Blanchard:

In the past a leader was a boss. Today's leaders
must be partners with their people. They can no longer
lead based on positional power.[8]

This is an iterative process, but also a different way of viewing the work of the C-suites and We-suites. In such a team or family, we all have responsibilities in the partnership to create constantly and then to keep the new creation functioning the way it is designed, "calling audibles" as necessary to change "the play," while staying constant to the Deep Joy to which we are mutually committed.

And never let diminutive stature or place in the organization become a false marker for the tenacity and capability of the team member, whether in the We-suite or the C-suite. One of the most trusted leaders in my medical center was Earl, the director of Environmental Services (often called *housekeeping*). Earl is perhaps the least imposing, yet most impressive person in the entire hospital, respected for his immense dignity and kindness, not his commanding, controlling demeanor. If we had not included Earl in our innovation process of redesigning the hospital bed control system that drives the hospital's entire profitability, it would have been doomed to failure, since EVS was the rate-limiting step. When it came to helping us determine the root cause of our problem, he was essential.

Yes, the C-suite should have a fanatical dedication to innovation, but also a fanatical level of trust that the We-suite is not only capable of devising the needed change but it is their essential role in innovation.

THE ROLE OF THE C-SUITE

> *If we open a quarrel between the past and*
> *the present, we shall surely lose the future.*
> WINSTON S. CHURCHILL[9]

It is not my intent to open a quarrel between the C-Suite and the We-suite. I realize that my words about the C-suite and the We-suite may be interpreted as offensive or even derisive . . . particularly to those in the C-suite. To the contrary, the members of the C-suite team play a critical role in every organization—*just not the role we have traditionally assumed.*

To rely on the C-suite to innovate systems and processes is simply absurd—it doesn't work, as history and experience have shown us. The people in the C-suite don't do the team's work every day, so how can they possibly know how to change the work to make the team's work easier and the lives of those we serve better? (And even if they previously did the work on the way to the C-suite, they no longer do it, they don't have the familiarity with it that they once might have had, and the work they previously did has changed—sometimes radically so.)

If all this is true—and it is—what are the legitimate roles of the C-suite?

- Foster a spirit of empowerment, innovation, and trust, in which the We-suite's creative energy leads to innovation at the speed of trust.
- Uncover the happenings in the halls defining our culture and assure that the words on the walls match them—not the other way around.
- Empower the We-suite to unleash innovation daily, not just when the strategic plan is hauled out and dusted off for review.
- Assure there are thin rulebooks and wide corridors for success.
- Eliminate my-way-or-the-highway mentalities.
- Create hope and the tools to leverage, expedite, and accelerate effective innovation—not produce the innovation themselves.
- Find ways to say "Yes" instead of "No" or "We tried that already . . ."
- Celebrate innovative successes . . . and failures.
- Find pathways to finance the desired innovations—show the return on investment.
- Make sure the other C-suite members are on board and a part of the onboarding process of innovation.

- Identify and celebrate creative, team-driven resistance.
- Hire right, train right, promote right.

And remember . . .

- What we permit we promote.
- What we allow we encourage.
- What we celebrate we accelerate.

THE ROLE OF THE WE-SUITE

So, now that we've determined what the legitimate roles of the C-suite are, that brings us to the natural next question: What are the legitimate roles of the We-suite? Here are some of the most essential:

- Follow your Deep Joy.
- Know your job.
- Do your job.
- But . . . lead in your job every day, creating culture and leaving a legacy while you follow your Deep Joy.
- Don't aspire to become a leader, embrace the fact you are a leader, and inspire others.
- But, also, and critically, do the job with a lens for the innovations that are essential for the future.
- Approach each day understanding that in addition to your job—regardless of what that job is—you have an additional responsibility: to assess how the job could be done differently to better serve others while making everyone's jobs easier.
- Communicate to the C-Suite what those innovations are, why they are *smart stuff*, and what the team will need to do to make that a reality.

And to be clear, this means we can no longer harbor a victim's mentality, where the C-suite is always to blame for our perils and travails. We must accept responsibility as team members that it is *our work to do,* augmented and assisted by the C-suite.

In the fall of 2001, when I became the NFL Players Association's first medical director, the first meeting I attended was at NFL Headquarters, then at 280 Park Avenue in New York City. The meeting was scheduled to start at 10:00 a.m.

At 9:55 a.m., Gene Upshaw and I were in the coffee shop around the corner and still had to get through security and be escorted upstairs. (I confess to a fixation on punctuality, as being late signals rudeness, at least from my point of view.) But Gene was in no hurry, laughing and joking with the barista, the security guards, and the secretaries along the way—completely oblivious of the time (and my discomfort . . .).

At exactly 10:12 a.m., we finally wandered into the Pete Rozelle Board Room, where we found 32 team physicians, 19 head athletic trainers, several lawyers, my then counterpart at the NFL—Dr. Elliot Pellman—and Paul Tagliabue, the commissioner of the NFL. On our side, it was just the three of us: Gene, Trace Armstrong (our union president), and me.

Gene gazed around the room and said, "We may be outnumbered, but we will *never* be outmanned!"

In leading your life in the active voice, you will often find yourself outnumbered . . . but don't ever let yourself be outmanned!

The C-suite may have you outnumbered in meetings—don't let them have you outmanned . . .

SUPER BOWL ADVICE

One of the duties of my job as the medical director of the NFL Players Association is to attend the Super Bowl every year, inspect the field, and assure that the medical equipment, paramedics, ambulances, helicopter, and other essential elements for the health and safety of our players are all in place and ready to go. (I know, tough job . . . but someone has to do it . . .)

An hour before the game, the medical staffs of both teams (including trainers), the referee, and all the physicians assigned to cover the game assemble to do a "60-minute meeting" to ensure that everyone knows precisely what their role will be in the event of an emergency.

At the end, the meeting is turned over to me for my remarks, which always reflect these thoughts:

> First, on behalf of the 2,500 active players of the National Football League, thank you all for your commitment to these fine men and the service you provide them. Professional football has a 100 percent injury rate, and we thank you for the excellent care you provide to them.
>
> Second, congratulations to both teams for your excellent season and to you, the medical staffs who got them here. Just as your players are Super Bowl quality, your medical staffs are as well, so we know how good you are.
>
> Third, relax, do your jobs as you always have and don't think about the fact that there are over 100 million people watching you! Just don't screw it up. Have fun and good luck.

It has been my honor and pleasure over the years to work with some of the best sports medicine physicians on the planet, including my friend Paul Cusick, MD, head team primary care physician for the New England Patriots, who recently retired. I wrote him a heartfelt note of thanks and congratulations for all his excellent work over the years. Here's what he wrote back:

> Thom, I am so grateful for your kind words. Your thoughtfulness means more to me than you can know.
>
> I have always admired your thoughtful approach to an amazingly challenging job. You are a tireless advocate for players, with fairness and mirth. Not the easiest needle to thread.
>
> Whether it was in my first Super Bowl in 2007–8 or my 6th in 2018–19, you'll never know how comforting your pre-Super Bowl medical advice was to me:
>
> "Don't F it up, boys."
>
> Warmest regards,
> Paul[10]

While the C-suite of the NFL and the NFLPA working together were the genesis of our evidence-based evaluation and treatment protocols, it is the We-suite of the team medical staffs who enact them—they are the ones entrusted with caring for our players. And I will always treasure Paul's note . . .

A CLOSING THOUGHT

This is highly paradoxical, but a curious insight emerges as we near the end of this chapter:

> Both the C-Suite and the We-Suite are priceless . . . just in
> radically different ways than we have thought!

With this refreshed lens toward the C- and We-suites, let's next consider the pervasive problem of sucking up.

THE C-SUITE AND THE WE-SUITE SUMMARY

- The Boss doesn't have what you want—but you do.
- Who will devise the innovations? The answer to "Who?" is "You!"
- With the new understanding of the role of the C-suite, it is no longer worthless . . . it is priceless . . . but in a different way than we thought.

6

DON'T SUCK UP . . . SUCK DOWN

If leaders say they discourage sucking up, why does it happen so often? We can see this very clearly in others. We just can't see it in ourselves.

—MARSHALL GOLDSMITH[1]

On the evening of September 11, 2001, as the sun set on that cataclysmic day—and with fires still raging in the aftermath of the terrible attacks—I wore my orange COMMAND PHYSICIAN vest and settled into the role assigned to me.

All my life, people have told me, directly or indirectly, explicitly or tacitly, bluntly or obliquely, how important it is to show deference to those in charge, to respect authority, to seek answers from above— or, to put it bluntly, to "suck up." It occurred to me on that dark night that we spend most of our lives learning to suck up. However, sucking up wasn't going to take me anywhere at the Pentagon on September 11, 2001. That day, I discovered what every effective leader must learn: "Sucking up is worthless . . . but sucking down is priceless."

But how can you tell the difference when you walk into an organization? You'll know when you're in a sucking-up organization because the people in them constantly look to The Boss and to the C-suite for answers. A sucking-down organization is the exact opposite—the people know that the fundamental answers are within and among *everyone*. The answers aren't in the C-suite, but in the *We-suite*.

Sucking-up leaders often have a beautiful strategy, usually developed with the assistance of the hottest consultants du jour. Sucking-down leaders reach down to people throughout the organization to discover the real, enacted strategy—the strategy that the team members see in action during daily operations.

Sucking up seeks *power*. Sucking down seeks *influence*.

Suck down, not up. Choose influence, not power.

A DEFINITION OF SUCKING UP

The poster child for sucking up is Eddie Haskell, Wally's friend in the late-1950s TV show, *Leave It to Beaver*. Eddie perpetually sucked up to Wally and the Beaver's mother: "Why, don't you look *lovely* today, Mrs. Cleaver! And all my friends think so, too!"

Everyone remembers the suck-ups they knew growing up and those in the workplace. And when these suck-ups are successful at ascending the leadership ladder in our own organization, we shake our heads in amazement and disbelief.

Sucking up consists of the fundamental belief that success, advancement, and the answers to our questions are somehow *above us* in the organization. What we seek is therefore not within us, but outside of us, at a level in the organization to which we have not yet risen. This leads specifically to the obsequious and cloying behaviors we traditionally associate with sucking up. As Goldsmith notes in the quotation that opens this chapter, "We can see this very clearly in others. We just can't see it in ourselves."

There is a certain appeal to the idea that, even if *we* don't know the answers, at least *someone* does. Sucking up is thus a natural consequence since it allows us to believe that, despite our confusion, there is clarity at some higher, more knowledgeable, more privileged level of the organization. Even if we do not have the answers, it strangely comforts us to believe that someone else does.

A TOUCH OF HARRY IN THE NIGHT

I have been deeply moved by Shakespeare's magisterial play *Henry V*, which relates the Hundred Years' War Battle of Agincourt, which began on October 25, 1415, Saint Crispin's Day. French forces outnumbered the English by 5 to 1, with rested troops and archers, battle-tested and eager to close with their British enemy.

The evening before the battle, King Henry, nicknamed "Harry," walks among his beleaguered men. Here's how Shakespeare describes it:

> *That every wretch, pining and pale before,*
> *Beholding him, plucks comfort from his looks;*
> *A largess universal, like the sun,*
> *His liberal eye doth give to every one,*
> *Thawing cold fear, that mean and gentle all*
> *Behold, as may unworthiness define,*
> *A little touch of Harry in the night.*
> *Henry V*, Act IV, Prologue[2]

The king did not *order* his men into battle, as befits what most would deem worthy of a king. He *influenced* them into battle with his "liberal eye," which "doth give to every one . . . a little touch of Harry in the night."

King Henry provides a great example of a suck-down leader—the kind of leader who consciously chose influence, not power. And if it's good enough for a Plantagenet king, shouldn't it good enough for *you*?

THE PROBLEM WITH SUCKING UP—IT OFTEN WORKS

One of the reasons sucking-up is so prevalent is that everyone likes a compliment—particularly The Boss. Whether it is the CEO, the project director, the parent, or the coach, people like to hear that they are doing well, their efforts are working, and they are liked and appreciated.

An additional reason that sucking up is found throughout our society is because it often works. Who do you think will be more likely to succeed and be promoted in an organization? A manager whose consistent message is positive? "Great job, you've done it again Boss!" Or a manager who consistently emphasizes negativity and limitations? "Well, our margins did improve, but not nearly as much as they could have."

The former is more likely in many organizations to get praise and promotions, while the latter is labeled as a charter member of the BMW club: Bitch, Moan, and Whine.

BUT SUCKING UP DOES HAVE ITS LIMITS

While sucking up may have its superficial attractions—and even the occasional financial, power, and other rewards—it also has inherent limitations.

Chief among them is the fallacy that the answers we seek are above us.

For all our cloying behaviors toward our superiors, that pursuit is fundamentally futile. Even if we are asking the right questions, we are looking in the wrong place. In the short term, this creates wasted energy and misdirection. In the long term, it can lead to feelings of anger, disappointment, and even betrayal, when we finally arrive in the C-suite, only to find that the answers we sought for so long aren't there.

A second limitation of sucking up is that it often leads to under-informed or misinformed decision-making, as we discussed in the previous chapter. Whenever we play "Guess what The Boss is thinking" and "Let's get there before they do," we are heading into a minefield of uncertainty and guesswork. And even if we do end up at approximately the "right place," we have nonetheless wasted time and energy in doing so. In addition, our destination is often not what we could have achieved had there been clarity of purpose and the ability to use our own innovation and creativity to navigate the journey instead of sucking up.

I worked for a time as a physician for the Indian Health Service for the Nimiipuu (Nez Perce) nation in Idaho. One of my patients was an older gentleman whose skill and knowledge of the Wallowa Mountains was legendary.

Early one morning, he took me on a journey through those mountains, to a place where there were no paths, only dense forest. Within minutes, I was separated from him, but only by a few yards. He cautioned me to stay very close to him in the Wallowa wilderness. He said, "My son"—he actually said that—"our paths must be the same. Even if you are off by only two or three degrees, if we travel far enough—and today we will travel very far—soon we will be unable to see or hear one another."

In an information-based society where progress is as fast as the electrons that connect our smartphones and computers to the world around us, it takes no time at all to travel far enough that we are "unable to see or hear one another," even if our paths are off by only two or three degrees. Sucking-up organizations are filled with situations and scenarios that incorporate two to three degrees of navigational error, which often lead to outcomes that result in 180 degrees of directional error.

The third and most important limitation of sucking up is that the culture it creates kills creativity and innovation. "Guess what The Boss wants" may seem to go well when The Boss likes what they see but watch out if you guess wrong. In such climates, employees are rightly reluctant to take risks and innovate fully and creatively, unless they have a clear sense of what The Boss is looking for. Even then, the product is not innovation—it's "coloring inside the lines," often using colors you wouldn't have chosen and can barely stand to look at.

Not surprisingly, the final limitation of sucking up is that it is ultimately demoralizing and frustrating to those who work within such organizations. When your value is assessed by how well you suck up, instead of by your skills, talents, insight, and creativity—even as you advance up the ladder—you lose even when you win. Whether you are the suck-up or the suckee, this is no way to live.

A DEFINITION OF SUCKING DOWN

Sucking down is the belief that the locus of power, knowledge, and meaning in an organization is throughout and within the organization, including our peers and those who rank below us in position or seniority. It is important to note that sucking down doesn't preclude looking above in the organization, only in doing so exclusively. Sucking down is essential for any organization that values diversity and inclusion since it draws on all perspectives.

Sucking down requires some very distinct skills, which include:

- Servant leading
- Listening strategically
- Humility and awareness of our own limitations
- Creating vision from chaos
- Encouraging innovation at the speed of trust

Let's take a few moments to review each of those skills.

SERVANT LEADING

If Eddie Haskell is the poster child for sucking up, then Robert K. Greenleaf is the patron saint of sucking down. Greenleaf introduced the concept of *servant leadership*, which recognizes that the most effective leaders are those who consciously seek to *serve first*, and only secondarily to *lead*. As Greenleaf observed about how to determine whether servant leadership is at work in an organization:

> *The best test, and the most difficult to administer is: Do those served grow as persons? Do they, while being served, become healthier, wiser, freer, more autonomous, more likely themselves to become servants?*[3]

A belief in servant leading is a belief in the power of sucking down. Sucking down leaders are interested first in *how people want to be served* and only secondarily in *how the leader wants to serve others*. Sucking down leaders (servant leaders) do not seek serenity or peace—

they already have it. What they seek is to help others achieve some measure of peace, while serving as their leader. That is their Deep Joy.

> Sucking down leaders are servant leaders—
> servants first and leaders second.

Let's return to King Henry and his men at Agincourt, as they prepared for battle against overwhelming odds. Here's what Henry said to his men, in Shakespeare's words:

> *This story shall the good man teach his son;*
> *And Crispin Crispian shall ne'er go by,*
> *From this day to the ending of the world,*
> *But we in it shall be remember'd;*
> *We few, we happy few, we band of brothers;*
> *For he today that sheds his blood with me*
> *Shall be my brother; be he ne'er so vile,*
> *This day shall gentle his condition:*
> *And gentlemen in England now a-bed*
> *Shall think themselves accursed they were not here,*
> *And hold their manhoods cheap whiles any speaks*
> *That fought with us upon Saint Crispin's day.*
> *Henry V*, Act IV, Scene 3

This is a perfect example of using intrinsic versus extrinsic motivation. King Henry appealed to his troops' sense of honor—their Deep Joy, if you will—of serving in a noble cause. He spurred them to overcome the obstacles arrayed before them, creating "we happy few," in stark contrast with those "gentlemen now a-bed" who "shall think themselves accursed they were not here."

This powerful king could have simply said, "I command you in the name of God and the throne to fight!" But he didn't . . . and they won, quickly and overwhelmingly, in fewer than three hours, making Agincourt a name that will live in honor forever.

That's servant leading in a time of crisis.

LISTENING STRATEGICALLY

In addition to a commitment to serve first, a fundamental attribute of a leader is the ability to listen strategically. However, sucking-down listening differs from sucking-up listening in two ways: *Who* you listen to and *how* you listen to them.

Sucking-up listening is primarily focused on those above them in the organization, including The Boss and their loyal band of suck-ups. Sucking-down listening reaches down in the organization as well as up, seeking to discover not just what The Boss wants, but what those we serve desire.

Sucking down leaders listen first, listen strategically, and listen actively. They understand what the great physician Sir William Osler meant when he said, "It is more important to know what sort of patient has the disease than what sort of disease the patient has."[4]

Osler's wisdom applies to many of our organizations today—leaders need to have a clear idea of "what sort of disease" our companies have before they can address their issues. They clearly understand strategic direction, mission statements, and profit and loss sheets. But they often lack an understanding of "what sort of patient has the disease," in that they fail to understand not only what sort of people populate the organization, but also lack any knowledge of the talents, aspirations, and dreams of those people.

When I found myself wearing the orange COMMAND PHYSICIAN vest at the Pentagon on what may well be one of the key defining days of our generation, the lessons I learned came not from listening *above* to generals and CEOs and other potentates. The lessons I learned came from listening *below*—to everyday people doing everyday jobs in extraordinarily challenging circumstances. For hours, it seemed that most of my sentences began:

"I need your help with this . . ."

"Help me understand this."

"What's your take on this?"

"I've got a tough decision—I need your input on . . ."

"How would you handle this problem?"

"This is your area of expertise, educate me . . ."

Gearing up with oxygen tank, mask, and protective headgear to go into the still-burning Pentagon on September 11 required a certain amount of courage, especially if you are as claustrophobic as I am. *But sucking-down listening also requires courage.*

Downward-reaching conversations are not intuitive, and it requires courage for the simple reason that many people expect the leader to already have the answers, not to be seeking them within and throughout the organization. My father, Grandpa Jim, wisely told me, "Son, it's not important to be important in life. But it's critically important to know important people." And the best way to know important people is to suck down . . .

Sucking-down listening hears *what is*, whereas sucking-up listening often discerns only *what is supposed to be.* For sucking-up organizations, understanding operations comes from perusal of operations manuals and volumes of policies and procedures. If leaders want to understand where the organization is headed, should they consult the strategic plan and quarterly goals and objectives? Or should they invest the time, energy, and effort to listen down and throughout the organization? It's your choice, but I think you know by now what I hope your answer will be.

Sucking-down listening also requires the uncommon self-confidence to know that when you expose your lack of knowledge on a particular topic, you actually enhance, not detract from your capacity to lead. Your vulnerability becomes your strength.

Take a moment to look at the six letters in this word:

LISTEN

Now think about how you could rearrange those same six letters in a way that provides deeper meaning, as well as a path to listen strategically. Take a moment or two to give this exercise a try . . .

Done? OK—here you go:

SILENT

Same letters, deeper meaning. And not to offend anyone, but we aren't very good at silence in our society. Pauses in conversation produce anxiety and are usually filled quickly. This is true even after we have asked someone a question, instead of looking at the person kindly, patiently, and waiting for their answer.

In medicine, both our team and Jerry Groopman at Harvard studied the ability to listen by remaining silent with our patients. We had medical students observe our conversations, armed with a stopwatch. On average, the amount of time that elapses from when a physician asks a patient a question, until they interrupt that patient's answer is . . .

18 seconds.

For nurses, it is at least a little better since their time to interruption is . . .

54 seconds.[5]

(When my wife Maureen, a former neonatal intensive care unit [NICU] flight nurse, heard these data, she said, "Well that just proves that nurses are three times better than doctors!")

Think about that—we ask our patient a question and then we barely let them finish a sentence! We need to work on that in medicine, but the same concept proves true no matter what we do. Cultivating the habit of listening strategically requires learning the value of silence.

Advocate as if you are certain you are *right* . . .
But *listen* as if you are certain you are *wrong.*

An example of the power of listening down instead of up comes from my own experience with the 2001 bioterrorism crisis in our nation's capital. Scarcely a month after the 9/11 tragedy, anthrax-laced letters were mailed to the Hart Senate Office Building. Within days, hundreds of patients (many of them postal workers) came to our emergency department desperately concerned that they might have anthrax.

At that time, we did what most people would—we listened to recognized authorities with demonstrated expertise in the area, in this case the Centers for Disease Control and Prevention (CDC). In other words, we practiced sucking-up listening.

What we heard were reassurances that unless you were in the Hart Senate Office Building on October 15, 2001, on the fifth and sixth floors of the southeast wing between 9:00 a.m. to 7:00 p.m., there was absolutely nothing to be concerned about.[6] Based on what was thought to be good science, the CDC declared that it wasn't possible unless you had been in that specific building on those specific floors at the time the letter was opened.

However, on October 19, 2001, a worker at the Brentwood postal facility in Washington by the name of Leroy Richmond arrived at our emergency department. He told the emergency physician who took his case, Dr. Cecele Murphy, "I think I have anthrax."

Listening upward—consulting the recognized authorities— would have resulted in her saying to this patient, "Don't worry, the experts say you're OK." Fortunately, Dr. Murphy didn't do that. She did what all great physicians do—she listened to the patient, who told her, "My chest feels very strange. I know my body, and something just doesn't feel right."

Dr. Murphy recognized Sir William Osler's wisdom, since she understood the importance of "what sort of patient has the disease." She learned that Mr. Richmond was very attuned to his body, and his body was telling him something was desperately wrong.

Dr. Murphy obtained a chest x-ray and then a more detailed CT scan of his chest, which revealed dramatic evidence of potentially fatal inhalational anthrax. Quite simply, even though Mr. Richmond did not appear acutely ill, in fact his chest was literally dissolving— and he was getting worse by the hour. (Even today, looking at the chest CT gives me cold chills.) Following Dr. Murphy's diagnosis,

Mr. Richmond was treated aggressively with antibiotics and survived his terrible illness.

Because Dr. Murphy listened down instead of up, Mr. Richmond and two other postal workers are alive today. Sucking down listening has its rewards.

During disasters, when communications need to be at their best, they are in fact often at their worst and most misinformed. Strategic listening helps prevent this because it is not unidirectional, but omnidirectional, listening within and throughout the organization. It produces *listening redundancy*, assuring that we hear information from multiple sources, in multiple voices, all of which must be interpreted and unified.

It also uses active listening, where those with whom we communicate are asked to repeat what we just said, and that we acknowledge them with, "Here's what I heard you say . . ." followed by "Did I get that right?" Dr. Murphy certainly considered the advice of the CDC, but she listened more closely to Mr. Richmond, even though he didn't fit the experts' description of anthrax. She didn't suck up to the CDC, she "sucked down" to the patient—and saved his life.

HUMILITY AND AWARENESS OF OUR OWN LIMITATIONS

In addition to possessing a servant's heart, empowered by strategic listening, those who suck down have a clear and guiding sense of humility regarding their own limitations, particularly when they are charged with leading. This requires a fundamental understanding that we are less in control of events than many people would like to think.

The focus of sucking-down leaders is thus not themselves and what they bring to the organization, but on what they can help others attain and accomplish. One fundamental question clarifies this:

Are those we serve lucky we are here?
Or are we lucky they are here?

Servant leaders know *they* are lucky *those we serve* are here . . .

Be sensitive to the trap of false humility. After hearing one of her cabinet ministers proclaim his humility, former Israeli Prime Minister Golda Meir remarked,

Don't be so humble . . . you're not that great.[7]

CREATING VISION FROM CHAOS

Perhaps the most elusive skill of the sucking-down leader is the ability to conceptualize vision from chaos and confusion, particularly when there are diverse opinions of what to do. Creating vision means the ability to see potential, non-evident order in the complexity and chaos, as well as communicating that vision in ways that resonate within the organization.

The "lead" in leader comes from what at times seems to be an uncanny foresight—the ability to anticipate *what* is going to happen *when* (often with incredible accuracy) based on a hyperacute sense of *now*, guided by a strong knowledge of history and human nature. In the sucking-up organization, conceptualizing vision isn't particularly important. Those organizations are too busy trying to guess what The Boss wants. In sucking-down organizations, however, the focus is on discovering this sense of vision throughout the organization.

Sucking up is relatively easy, since all you need to do is to discover what The Boss wants and then execute. Sucking down is more difficult. Not only do you have to find the patience and time to strategically listen to different viewpoints; you must have the skill to meaningfully integrate these different viewpoints. This is tough work. And it's confusing. As the physicist Niels Bohr said, "The opposite of a correct statement is a false statement. But the opposite of a profound truth may well be another profound truth."[8]

Ferreting out profound truths and communicating them meaningfully as the opposite of another profound truth is tough business, and it wears you out. Conceptualizing and communicating vision involves the ability to gain a perspective "above the action," to see which path to take, and the talent to communicate the vision through storytelling.

ENCOURAGING INNOVATION AT THE SPEED OF TRUST

Innovation occurs at the speed of trust. Sucking-down leaders encourage experimentation and innovation, offering a wide zone of tolerance for creativity in a culture permeated by trust.

Sucking-down leaders understand Maslow's insight that the highest level of hierarchy of needs is self-actualization, and that self-actualization is fueled by creativity. This creativity does not come from the top, but from within the organization, catalyzed by sucking-down (servant) leaders. Those who meaningfully (not just cosmetically) tap into this creativity not only develop a competitive edge, but they also cultivate a new, rising group of servant leaders.

Many of us use the lack of rank or power as an excuse for our failure to create, innovate, and experiment. Sucking down removes that excuse. No longer can you blame The Boss for doing mediocre work, or delivering lousy products. Sucking down helps encourage and nourish experimentation by creating an expectation that diverse, varied, and contrarian ideas are not only tolerated, but encouraged.

The sucking-down leader assures that a culture exists where servant leading encourages such expertise and experimentation to rise. The rewards of learning to suck down in a world full of suck-ups are many, including creativity, adaptability, speed of change, innovation, and reliability. But chief among these rewards is that work is just a lot more fun.

As terrible as the Pentagon and bioterrorism crises of 2001 were, there was simply no question among those of us who were privileged to serve that this was *our* job to do. Emergency physicians, firefighters, paramedics, and police have a neural programming "fault." When planes crash into buildings or when death comes through the mail, normal people choose the sensible path—they run away. We don't. We run *into* fire, smoke, and danger.

We did the same when my Team Rubicon Mobile Emergency Team went to Ukraine when the war broke out. We weren't required to do it but we chose to do it. Why? Because we obtained tremendous satisfaction from caring for people who no one else would. It is where our Deep Joy intersected the world's deep needs.

Prior to his career as a distinguished psychoanalyst, Viktor Frankl was imprisoned in several different Nazi concentration camps, including Theresienstadt. In his book, *Man's Search for Meaning*, he made the somewhat curious observation that he was never freer than when he was imprisoned. Said Frankl, "Everything can be taken from a man but one thing: the last of the human freedoms—to choose one's attitude in any set of circumstances, to choose one's own way."[9]

Because it was in those camps that Frankl learned that we can never control what happens to us in life, but we can *always* control how we feel about it and how we react to it. No one can do that but us.

> *The impossible we do immediately.*
> *The miraculous takes a little longer.*
> Lt. General Brehon Somervell[10]

So, what kind of leader will you be? Will you spend your time sucking up or sucking down? Fundamentally, it is your choice to make. But don't be surprised if, in choosing to be a sucking-down leader, you find that the miraculous, as General Somervell said, "takes a little longer." When you make that choice, you make the impossible possible and the miraculous likely.

OUT OF THE MOUTHS OF ORPHANS

Josh, our oldest son, and then a senior at Dartmouth College, spent several months volunteering at El Hogar, an orphanage in Honduras, where the conditions were stark at best. His reflections on the experience are emblematic of the humility of the sucking-down leader:

> One of the most important lessons I learned is that what I brought to El Hogar was very little compared to *what the boys brought out of themselves when allowed.* The most valuable gift the program gives to the boys is an assurance of their own worth and dignity in a world that, all too often, has only sent them messages to the contrary.[11]

SUCKING DOWN FOR OUR NFL PLAYER-PATIENTS

The genesis of the so-called NFL Concussion Protocol and the Un-affiliated Neurotrauma Consultant programs are testament to our commitment to listening to the voice of the player-patient (sucking down) instead of deferring to the voice of the potentates of the NFL (sucking up).

In 2011, we (the NFLPA) proposed evidence-based concussion protocols to protect our players against the wide variation in how concussed players were diagnosed and treated. Sean Sansiveri, general counsel and head of business affairs for the union, and I drafted the first concussion protocols, which were initially strongly resisted by the team physicians and the NFL. Despite the NFL's power, the protocols were adopted and are arguably the best in all sports. More important, we changed the entire culture of concussion—not only in the NFL, but throughout contact sports. In this very important case, the influence of the voice of the player-patient exceeded the power of the NFL.

In 2014, we proposed expanding the concussion program with the addition of unaffiliated neurotrauma consultants (UNC)—board-certified experts in neurotrauma who were independent of the teams and who had significant experience in head trauma. Again, we encountered resistance. The team physicians and the then co-chairs of the NFL's Head, Neck, and Spine Committee (HNS) strongly opposed this initiative. The issue was decided in a joint conference call between the NFL Players Association and the NFL, represented by the HNS co-chairs, several of its members, and team physicians.

To represent the player-patients on this call, we chose Sean, me, and two players who were highly respected by the NFL's representatives—Ernie Conwell, a former tight end and H-back, and Domonique "Fox" Foxworth, then the president of our union and a Ravens All-Pro cornerback.

The league's representatives began the call by presenting their case for why the UNC program wasn't needed and how it would interfere with the team physicians' ability to practice medicine.

I turned it over to the players, saying, "Ernie, Fox, you are the voice of the player-patient—what's your take?"

Ernie went first, with his remarks aimed squarely at the neuro-surgeons on the call.

"Doc, I don't understand this. As an NFL player, you give me one orthopedist for my left knee, another one for my right shoulder, and a third for my hand. But you can't give me one for my *brain*?"

Into the stunned silence, Fox chuckled, "Yeah, and it isn't like you can't afford it!"

The deal was done immediately, and the program has remained in effect, with constant, iterative updates as the science of concussion evolves. And the genesis of the program came not from the power of the NFL, but the influence of the voice of the player-patient. Instead of sucking up to the powerful NFL, we sucked down with the voices of our players.

Choose influence over power because the ultimate power is the voice of those you are privileged to serve.

Now, let's turn to the importance of words versus actions in de-fining the culture and character of a team, which is the subject of the next chapter.

DON'T SUCK UP . . . SUCK DOWN SUMMARY

- The answers aren't *above* you, they are *within and among you.*
- Sucking up is demoralizing, demonic, and diminishing.
- Sucking down is enlightening, encouraging, and empowering.
- Will you be a suck-up or a suck-down leader? Make your choice . . .

7

SLOGANS ARE
WORTHLESS . . .
BUT ACTIONS
ARE PRICELESS

*Do not say things. What you are stands over you and
thunders so I cannot hear what you say to the contrary.*

—RALPH WALDO EMERSON[1]

In our emergency department, we had three of the most positive, proactive, and personable people on our team—Felicia, Fannie, and
Bernardo—who worked in housekeeping or EVS (environmental
services, previously called "janitors," a term which has mercifully
been relegated to the dustbin of history . . .). Without fail, they had
smiles, kind words, a gentle touch, and always went the extra mile to
be helpful, often staying over at the end of the shift if they were needed.

The hospital decided to launch a customer service campaign, and
they hired a consulting company and spent a lot of shekels in the
process. No one outside the C-suite had any input into the process
until the chairs and heads of departments were summoned to an

unveiling of the new campaign. With much excitement and fan-fare, those responsible for the initiative brought the event to its in-evitable climax, presenting the assembled group of leaders with a bevy of motivational posters—not unlike Moses bringing those fa-bled commandments down from the mountaintop.

To be honest, I can't recall what those slogans said, since they were so unimpressive that they verged on condescending. The CEO asked, "Doc, you don't look excited about this—what's on your mind?"

Before I could restrain myself, I heard myself respond, "Why didn't you just put up a picture of Felicia, Fannie, and Bernardo with a caption 'Thanks to our Customer Service Heroes?'" (Secretly, I thought, "Hey I can always find another job . . .")

Stunned silence followed, but the CEO pondered my response for a moment. He then turned to the team and said, "Go get a picture of Felicia, Fannie, and Bernardo!"

Better to have a handful of passionate champions who know their Deep Joy and how it intersects the world's deep needs than 1,000 slo-gans proclaiming it.[2]

We've all seen motivational posters like the ones presented in the conference room that day, sometimes seemingly everywhere, scream-ing their messages to us in the middle of a stressful day: "Courage!" "Perseverance!" "Stick-to-it-iveness!" "Have a Nice Day!"

On bad days, it seems like they are taunting us, describing our deficiencies, and reminding us how much better others are.

If I have to look up at a slogan on the wall to figure out what to do . . . something is *seriously* wrong.

More important, I have rarely seen a motivational poster or slo-gan campaign designed by the people actually doing the work. It al-ways seems to be The Boss's or the C-suite's idea—the people farthest away from the organization's work and its customers. Regardless, many if not most businesses have them, as if they were indispensable to keeping teams from running the company into a ditch. Even multi-billion-dollar tech giants like Facebook use them, famously plaster-ing motivational posters with the exhortations, "What Would You Do

If You Weren't Afraid?" "Move Fast and Break Things," "Fortune Favors the Bold," and more on the walls of its many offices worldwide.[3]

If I want to know what the culture and the values of your company are, don't show me your posters and slogans. Instead, give me just ten minutes to observe your team in action. At the end of those ten minutes, I'll tell you precisely what your culture and values are. Remember . . .

Culture = Actions = Leading

In the quotation that opens this chapter, Emerson expresses a wisdom too often forgotten in our work and family lives. Culture is what we *do,* not what we *say.* Culture is result of the cumulative actions each of us undertakes during our day. Not only do we create a new culture each day (or sustain one whose foundation we laid in previous days), we also create a culture in every interaction in which we are involved. Every time I see one of my players or a patient in the ER, my team and I create a unique culture with that individual in the moment.

We don't have to *tell* each other what our culture is—we *enact* a culture in every action, since leading is action, particularly interaction with our teammates, those we serve, and our families. The sooner we accept that, the sooner and better we can leave a legacy. (More on leaving a legacy later in this chapter . . .)

Because it's not the slogans on the walls that matter . . . it's the actions in the halls.

MISSION, VISION, AND VALUES STATEMENTS VS. HAPPENINGS IN THE HALLS

I am a big believer in organizational mission, vision, and values statements—with a few key provisos and caveats.

First, all great mission, vision, and values statements I have seen were *uncovered or discovered* by tapping into the hearts and minds of those doing the work to see what motivates them and sustains *them.* Too often, the *toll extracted* from the systems and processes in which we work are not matched by the *benefits enacted* for us as we serve our customers, patients, and families. Watching a team at work shows us the seams of the team and how they can navigate towards success.

One of the great humorists of our times, Mel Brooks, captures this idea perfectly in *History of the World, Part 1,* when he portrays Moses descending from Mount Sinai, carrying three stone tablets and proclaiming, "The Lord Jehovah has given unto you these 15 . . ." As Moses says these words, one of the tablets slips from his grasp and crashes to the ground, smashing to pieces. Moses looks down at remnants of the broken tablet and quickly says, "Oy—10, 10 Commandments for all to obey!"[4] Irreverent, to be sure, but sometimes posters and slogans have the same forceful commands—yet seem arbitrary or even capricious.

Second, and completely unsurprisingly, the genesis and successive iterations of the statements should involve those doing the work—the *We-suite.* These people know better than anyone else what works and what doesn't, as well as who the A Team and B Team members are and their various attributes. Give them a voice in articulating the mission, vision, and values, or at a minimum, the permission to speak freely when the systems and processes are getting in the way of their doing a good job. And if your family generates a mission statement, do it as a family—not on your own as a high-and-mighty patriarch or matriarch.

Third, does the poster or slogan *empower* or *lecture* the team? Is it devised with the team's input and with a clear lens that sharpens their view on the benefits enacted to the customer—and to themselves—in doing the work? Or is it yet another version of Big Brother gazing over their shoulders, attempting to ensure that they don't screw up, while assuming that is precisely what they would do if left to their own inclinations?

Does it inspire people to lead, and while leading, serve others? If not, then I suggest that these exhortations aren't worth the paper they're printed on.

Finally, once the mission, vision, and values tap into the Deep Joy of the team, are those guiding forces used to hire right, meaning are people exposed to them during the process of joining the team? *Hire right* reflects the fact that hiring is the most important—and potentially, the most expensive—decision a team will ever make.[5] This is the case because hiring the *wrong* team member can be tremendously devastating to morale and results, as well as to the bottom line. And then replacing a team member who doesn't fit can be an even more expensive, time-consuming, and demoralizing process as candidate after candidate fails to impress.

The same is true of families. While we don't hire the members of our family in the traditional sense, we can re-recruit and retrain them to whatever the family's vision is, as well as the people comprising the family.

If the mission, vision, and values are lyrical enough for us all to endorse and embrace, they should be widely known to those who seek to join the team. Further, *hire right* should mean discussing this with the prospective team members and advising them that if they disagree or can't embrace the core values and the mission and vision, this might not be the best team to join. Better to join a team whose values match yours than condemn yourself—and the team—to a long winter of discontent.

THE POWER OF EMPOWERMENT

None of the great leaders I have personally known or studied succeeded without empowering their team members. But what does that word *empowerment* mean? To me, like most things, it is far simpler than many have made it.

Empowerment simply means driving decisions down to the levels at which the work is done, and entrusting the team to decide the details of how the work is to be completed.

The corollary is that those who do the work are also charged with constantly and iteratively redesigning the work they do to adapt to the fast-changing world in which we live and do business today.

The very best leaders refrain from looking over the team's shoulder, constantly nitpicking the ways in which things are done and driving them to distraction. In addition, the very best leaders not only recognize that every other team member is a leader, but that they know *their work* at a different level and are therefore more likely to know how to fix it. Unsurprisingly, I believe that empowerment of necessity requires *entrusting* the team or the family to not only do the right things, but to think, act, and innovate in creative ways.

What kind of teams do you lead? Are they thin-rulebook or thick-rulebook teams? And do you give them wide or narrow corridors of success? Let's explore these four different kinds of teams.

THIN-RULEBOOK TEAMS VS. THICK-RULEBOOK TEAMS

The team-generated mission, vison, and values must be clearly known by every member of the team. But once these things are known, do you have a thick rulebook, to which the team or family must retreat to know what to do, looking up every detail on how to get it right? Or do you have a thin rulebook, one that states general principles and entrusts the details to an empowered team? Believe me, the latter is better than the former every time.

Create thin-rulebook teams.

WIDE-CORRIDORS-FOR-SUCCESS TEAMS VS. NARROW-CORRIDORS-FOR-SUCCESS TEAMS

When you work with your teams, do you give them wide corridors for success, where there are many different ways to succeed from which they can choose? Or do you give them only narrow corridors for success, where it's "My way or the highway?"

Create wide-corridors-for-success teams.

Several years ago, I had the opportunity to work with a large, highly respected healthcare system. Despite their venerable reputation, they were not getting the results from their team that they expected. And it's no wonder—the team was described as "demoralized and disorganized." When speaking to several hundred people in the main auditorium, I asked this question, "Are you empowered?"

In the silence that followed, a small voice ventured from the back of the room:

"They tell *us we are . . ."*

Is your team empowered? Or are you just telling people they are . . .

LOOKING UP VS. LOOKING WITHIN

Every day, in every interaction, we choose what culture we will create in leading through actions, since (with a nod to Aristotle) we are what we repeatedly do. Sometimes it's relatively obvious what to do, but often it is more obscure.

When that happens, do you have to look up at the poster to figure out the right path (the words on the walls)? Or do you look where the answers truly lie—*within* yourself and your teammates?

Don't look up the answers for what path to choose—look within. You shouldn't have to look at a poster to tell you what to do.

Say to yourself . . .

"I am going to create my culture today."

"How will we create our culture?"

"We just created our culture."

"How did we create culture today?"

"How can we create an even better culture tomorrow?"

If you choose empowerment—and you should—empower yourself first. Then empower your team. They will empower those you serve, whether patients, customers, or family members. It's like the safety brief flight attendants repeat from memory whenever your plane is about to take off: "In the event of a sudden loss of cabin pressure, oxygen masks will automatically drop from the ceiling. Grab the mask and pull it over your face. If you have children traveling with you, secure your mask before assisting with theirs."

First, empower yourself, then empower your team.

THE ROLE OF COACHING AND MENTORING
IN AN EMPOWERED CULTURE

It's important to recognize the critical role that coaching and mentoring play in an empowered culture. While The Boss coaches and mentors with a top-down approach, the leader focuses not on what went wrong, but what went right—and critically, how both success and failure occurred.

Remember the story about Patriots coach Scar and Super Bowl LI? When his team seemed destined to lose, with the score 28–3 in favor of the Falcons, Coach Scar removed the levers that the Falcon edge rushers used to pressure Tom Brady in the first half. The result was the first overtime win in Super Bowl history, with a final score of 34–28 for the Patriots.

While Brady and the rest of the team all pulled together to win the championship, much credit must go to Coach Scar's ability—and willingness—to dig deep into what was and wasn't working, then making corrections that had a direct impact on the outcome.

So, coach and mentor—and be ready to be coached and mentored yourself. Focus not just on what went wrong, but also on <u>how</u> it went wrong and what to do to make it right next time.

When our boys were younger, I was happy to coach their sports teams, but only when they asked me. I understand parents as coaches can be the dirty little secrets of youth sports, acting out their own unfulfilled ambitions—often screaming and yelling at the poor kids, in their best imitations of Vince Lombardi or Bobby Knight. I took a different approach, focusing not on win-loss records, but on talent and character development. (And remembering Coach Bill Belichick's wisdom that while talent sets the floor of a team, character sets the ceiling.)

As the season started for one of these teams that I coached, I had a meeting with the assistant coaches and parents. I told them that having fun and developing character were our goals, through a better mastery of skills:

The coaches won't be telling your sons that they did something wrong—we will tell them *how* it went wrong and *how to make it right.* That builds confidence and character. And when we huddle with the whole team before and after every practice and every game, we will all yell the same thing every time: 'First in fun!' If anyone is uncomfortable with that, I'll be happy to arrange for a trade to another team.

Despite a few initial discomfited looks from some parents, no one ever asked for a trade.

Years later, when I see those kids—now young men—they always give me a smile and yell, "First in fun!"

FIRST IN FUN!

You met Coach John Danowski, Duke Men's Lacrosse coach, in Chapter 3. In the opening round of the 2023 NCAA Men's Lacrosse Tournament, the Duke Blue Devils were ranked number 1 and were the top seed in the tournament. No top-seeded team had ever lost in the first round of the tourney, but the Blue Devils trailed Delaware at halftime 8–5 and nothing was going right. But in the second half they chipped away at the lead, finally winning 12–11 at the end.

After the game, reporters asked Coach Dino what he told the team at halftime. He responded:

> I think every team has a crucible moment, where you're looking into the abyss a little bit. At halftime, they just weren't having fun. And it's still a game and it's about having fun. That was the mantra at halftime, "Fellas, whatever happens here in the last 30 minutes on this field, let's have fun!"[6]

First in fun, indeed!

And for those for whom keeping score is more important than developing character and confidence, we won a lot more games than we lost . . .

LEAVING A LEGACY

When most people hear the term *legacy*, they think of something that they'll leave for their children or future generations. I personally think of legacy in a fundamentally different, more actionable way:

> Every day, with every action in which we lead,
> we not only create a culture—we also leave a legacy.

Think of your legacy like the riprap I mentioned in the Introduction to this book. Your legacy is comprised of all the actions you take throughout your life, and over time, they become the interlocking stones that mark your path from the day you are born to the day you take your last breath.

Your actions in life, like the stones that become your path, should be chosen and laid with care instead of just randomly strewn about with no rhyme nor reason. And like breakwaters, which protect us from the vagaries of storms, our actions create a legacy of trust, so that we and our teams are protected from the inevitable obstacles we encounter as we lead in times of crisis.

In the profession of medicine, we are hugely fortunate in that we create a legacy by our actions one _____ at a time. But how do we fill in that blank?

For us, the joy is that we can build a legacy . . . *one patient at a time*. What an honor, what a privilege, what a great calculus by which we can measure our legacy. The same is true of you, regardless of your work and even within your own family—through every action, every day, all day.

What is the legacy *you* are leaving today? What actions are you taking, what stones are you carefully selecting to pave your way?

And speaking of legacy, on Memorial Day weekend at Lincoln Financial Field in Philadelphia, Coach Danowski's Duke Blue Devils played in the NCAA Finals against the Notre Dame Fighting Irish.

Despite falling behind 6–1 at halftime, they roared back to tie the game in the fourth quarter but lost in a nailbiter. When Coach was asked by reporters what he told his team after the game, he smiled and said, "I told them, 'Men, if this is the worst thing that happens to you in life . . . you are living a really great life!'" That's a legacy worth having . . . And on July 1, 2023, as coach of the US National Team, Coach Danowski became the only coach in history whose teams won consecutive World Championships.

Please do what I tell my healthcare teams to do . . . At the end of the day—before heading home, but after you start your car or step on the bus or train—pause for a moment and ask yourself, "What legacy did I leave in there today?"

Now, do the same in your life, and you may find on reflection that you left a greater legacy than you might have thought. Your legacy is far less about the words on the walls you left behind than on the happenings in the halls you created.

And remember the 3 Good Things exercise. Be kind to yourself by remembering your role in creating those three legacies.

In the next chapter, we'll discuss why—despite the importance of the right word—it is stories, not words, that are priceless.

SLOGANS ARE WORTHLESS . . . BUT ACTIONS ARE PRICELESS SUMMARY

- It's not the words on the walls, but the happenings in the halls that matter.
- It is our actions, what we *do*, that defines us, our teams, and our cultures.
- Culture = Actions = Leading
- Make sure the *benefits enacted* exceed the *toll extracted* in all we do.
- Leave a legacy.

8

THE HEALING POWER
OF THE STORY

All sorrows can be borne if you can put them into a
story or tell a story about them.

ISAK DINESEN NÉE KAREN VON BLIXEN[1]

On the afternoon of September 11, 2001, I was summoned to the Pentagon to act as the Command Physician of the Pentagon Rescue and Recovery Operation, in charge of the medical supervision and safety of the 5,000 firefighters, paramedics, heavy rescue, urban search and rescue, and FBI Evidence Recovery Teams on site. I was there into the chilly overnight hours, under the massive lights illuminating the site and in the shadows of the still burning building,

That night I saw two firefighters jury-rigging an American flag on the Pentagon firetruck located next to where American Airlines Flight 77 had struck the southwest wall of the building—causing the truck to burn down to its frame. As they struggled to attach the flagpole to the incinerated truck, I was reminded of the famed Joe Rosenthal photograph of US Marines planting the flag on Iwo Jima's Mount Suribachi (the photo upon which the Marine Corps Memorial is based, located just over a mile from the Pentagon). I instantly knew what had to be done.

I radioed the Army major detailed to handle public relations at the site to meet me, where I told him, "Sir, we have to find the biggest American flag which can be found and make sure it is on that wall next to the impact zone. We need a symbol which tells the world: 'You can burn our buildings and kill our people . . . but you can never kill the American spirit!'"

The next day, just as President George W. Bush and Secretary of Defense Donald Rumsfeld arrived at the Pentagon to shake the hand of every person on the site, the iconic Stars and Stripes was unfurled on the Pentagon's damaged wall (see exhibit 1), while everyone saluted and cheered. It became one of the most downloaded photos of September 11, 2001.

Using the power of stories is priceless, transforming sterile facts into meaning. Without the story, that's just a picture of a flag . . . But the right words are the building blocks of stories well told.

Mark Twain, as always, got it right in his emphasis on "the right word," and we do well when we remember that, editing constantly to find the elusive word:

> There is plenty of acceptable literature which deals largely in approximations, but it may be likened to a fine landscape seen through the rain; the right word would dismiss the rain, then you would see it better. It doesn't rain when Howells is at work.[2]

Don't let it rain when you are at work telling stories.

One of the most powerful lessons I have learned during the long course of my career is that it is *stories,* not simply the *words* comprising them, that allow us to take meaning from the world around us to guide our actions as they illuminate the way. The redemptive, healing power of stories cannot be overstated. The healing process sets off a balletic cascade of strengthening and renewing. The same is true for stories . . .

My advice has always been . . .

Don't just write words.

Don't just write sentences.

Exhibit 1. The American Flag unfurled on the wall of the Pentagon
following the 9/11 attack. Photograph by the author.

Don't just write paragraphs.

Don't just write chapters.

Write stories.

The most powerful stories are about people whose challenges, travails, hopes, aspirations, and failures we recognize—otherwise we attach little or no significance to them. My friend and colleague George Atallah is the assistant executive director of External Affairs for the NFL Players Association, a title that scarcely does justice to the magical way in which he crafts and communicates our messaging on behalf of our players.

Magic happens when George is at work . . .

WHO SHOULD YOUR STORIES BE ABOUT?

About whom should your stories be told? W. H. Auden provides us with an answer to that question in the opening lines of his poem "Musee des Beaux Arts":

> *About suffering, they were never wrong*
> *The Old Masters*
> *How well they understood*
> *Its human position . . .* [3]

Choose the right word but make the story about those we serve and the teammates who serve them, about those being led and those who lead them. Auden got it precisely right—seek to describe the "human position." The stories we tell about those we serve, whether patients, customers, or family members, should always be tales of *action*, of how leading allows us to better serve and lead others, as we enact our Deep Joy.

In my travels, I always get asked this question about leading in times of crisis:

> *What was it like leading through . . .*
> *the Pentagon on 9/11?*
> *the Anthrax Bioterrorism attack?*
> *the NFL Concussion Crisis?*
> *the Covid Pandemic?*
> *Ukraine?*
> *The Damar Hamlin miracle?*

The answer is simple.

The path to the head leads through the heart.

Tell the story of leading yourself as you lead your team and the emotion will come through on its own. This then influences the intellect deeply and significantly. Develop this one habit of leading and you will never go wrong:

Become the Chief Story Teller

BECOME THE CHIEF STORY TELLER

The stories you tell should always reflect the human position, the people you serve and those who help them. That's the thing—we are drowning in data in our organizations today. We're immersed in customer data, employee data, financial data, operational data, marketing data, sales data and on and on. But here's a secret: it's not the data that moves others to act—it's the *story*, which reflects what the data *mean* and how those data impact *people*.

Too often we know what we want to say, but less about how to make it have meaning, particularly meaning causing others to lead in the active voice. As an emergency physician and sports medicine doc, my patients come to me with symptoms, from chest pain to extremity trauma to lacerations . . . and everything in between. They know what happened to them . . . but they rely on me and my team to tell them *what it means.*

WHAT IT MEANS VS. WHAT IT SAYS

When our middle son Kevin was around ten years old, I came home from work in the evening to find him laboring at his English homework. Because he looked frustrated, I asked, "Kevin, do you want some help?"

"Yes, Dad, please." I read the passage he was working on and said, "Kevin, this is what it says."

Frustrated, Kevin threw down his pencil and said, "Dad, I know what it *says*—what does it *mean*!?"

To do that requires the skill and expertise of the Chief Story Teller, making meaning out of simple facts, inspiring them to lead through action. Mark Twain got it right when he said:

> *If you want a meteoric rise to the literary heights,*
> *don't write about Man . . .*
> *Write about "a man."*[4]

The story should always be about *people*, not abstract, ethereal ideas. And yes, use the right words when you tell those stories. Here is Twain again on that:

> *The difference between the right word and nearly the right*
> *word is the difference between lightning and a lightning bug,*
> *or a horse chestnut instead of a chestnut horse.*[5]

THE HABITS OF STORYTELLING

What are the habits of effective storytelling? While there are guidelines for effective storytelling, there are no hard and fast rules. But keep in mind that we humans are hardwired for stories—it's an integral part of our DNA and has been for countless millennia. The habits of storytelling date from well before the earliest recorded history and were instrumental in how knowledge and wisdom were shared from person to person and across generations. Storytellers were venerated as a vital repository of oral wisdom, tradition, and culture.

For example, in the West African Mali and Mande societies of the early fourth century, the *griot* (also known as a "jeli" or "jali") was the person who was entrusted with the collective wisdom of the village, but with the charge that he must pass this wisdom down through storytelling.[6] Through the centuries, every society and the religions that influenced them understood the importance of stories and the art of storytelling. And it's no accident that I tell many stories through the pages of this book to illustrate and amplify the point I make. Stories are powerful—they activate our minds and bodies and call us to action. A story well told sets off enzymatic reactions that guide us to action.

Here are some thoughts and observations about the art of story-telling I have learned along the way that might be helpful as you craft your own:

- Become a *student of storytelling*—figure out what works, what doesn't and why?

- As an astute observer of the stories of the human condition, don't just *watch*, make sure you *observe*—just as a scientist does—paying attention to the details of interactions, language, and behavior.

- Make your audience *care*—when telling or listening to a story, you are using a precious resource, one that cannot be stored, put on a shelf for later use, or ever recaptured. That precious resource is *time*. When you tell a story, use the listener's time well.

- Be willing to *ask* those with whom you are interacting what their issues are, including details on their intent, their message, and their underlying motivations.

- Use *active listening,* repeating back to others, "Here's what I *heard* you say—did I get that right?" or "I hear you—is that what you meant?

- When it's time to tell the story, whether verbally or in writing, *open your heart*. Your heart will tell you what to say and how to say it.

- In my view, the only reason to write or talk is to help someone. Is the story you're telling *helpful to others*—or is it loaded with a barb, a sting intended to harm. If so, it's probably a good idea not to say or write it.

- Pause, reflect, and reconsider, ask "Is this what I want or need to say?" Hone the story, excising extraneous details that don't firmly fix the people in the moment.

- Use humor whenever possible. Mark Twain was a master of that (and there is a reason the Kennedy Center's prize for humor is named "The Mark Twain Prize").

- That said, be cautious of sarcasm and its inherent cynicism.
  Our youngest son Greg is the kindest most thoughtful
  person I know, who says, "Don't make fun of people—you
  don't know what they are going through." Use self-
  deprecating humor.

- When others are the storyteller, listen closely, especially when
  they are captivating and moving you in ways that matter. Why
  is that? How is that person weaving the tale so well?

- Conversely, when someone is telling a story poorly, analyze
  why and how it has gone wrong. When it's your turn, don't
  make the same mistakes. Great storytellers learn from bad
  storytellers.

- Great stories build tension by pulling the listener in, helping
  them see around the corner . . . but not the final lines
  precisely. Help them arrive at the right place.

- Finally, remember what our son Kevin asked me, "What does
  it *mean?*" What meaning are you trying to convey and what
  action are you suggesting people take because of the story.

STORIES, PARABLES, METAPHOR, AND ALLEGORY

In the Introduction to his magisterial book *Legends of Our Time*,
Nobel Prize winner Elie Wiesel described a conversation he had with
the Rabbi (Rebbe) of his childhood.

When the Rebbe asked Elie what he was writing, he told him he
was writing stories—"true stories." When pressed further, however,
Elie explained to the Rebbe that the stories were about "people I might
have known" and about things that "could have happened." Elie continued, "In fact, some were invented from almost the beginning to almost the end."

The Rebbe replied, "That means you are writing lies!"

After a moment's reflection, Wiesel replied, "Things are not that
simple Rebbe. Some events do take place but are not true; others are,
although they never occurred."[7]

Parables, metaphors, and allegory may not have occurred, but they can all be effective means of communicating a story. When I talk to patients and families in the intensive care unit, I use the metaphor that what they are experiencing is a roller coaster ride, with breathtaking ups, and precipitous downs, yet ultimately arriving at the right place. They always thank me, telling me it was precisely like that for them.

For allegory—a story that uses symbolic representations of truths about human existence—one cannot surpass the model of the greatest allegorical poem of all time, Dante's *The Divine Comedy*, the opening lines of which are:

> *In the middle of the road of my Life*
> *I awoke in a Dark Wood*
> *Where the True Way was wholly lost*
> *Death could scarce be more bitter*
> *But if I would show the good that came from it*
> *I must talk about things other than the good.*[8]

If we want to help others out of the "Dark Wood" in which they are lost, allegorical stories can be effective.

STORYTELLING AND PASSION

Make the story come alive. If it excites you, it will excite your audience and if it bores you, it will surely bore your audience too. Never tell a story tentatively. Martin Buber often wrote about the Baal Shem Tov (literally "Master of the Good Name"), the founder of Hasidic thought, and told the story:

> The Baal Shem was lame. But he told a story about the importance of passion, illustrating it by speaking of a man so possessed by faith that it drove him to feverishly dance around the room. As the Baal Shem told the story, he rose and began to dance around the room himself, no longer lame. That's the way to tell a story.[9]

Tell your stories with passion and you won't be lame. Inspiration, epiphany, and passion often intersect—and when they do, cataclysmic change may occur. Stories, passionately told, not only change thoughts, attitudes, and words, they inspire actions, people leading other people in the active voice to change the world . . .

"I AM GEORGE FLOYD!"

Everything changed in just three days . . . The entire viewpoint of the NFL regarding race and social justice reversed course in just three days. It started with an Instagram DM. On Wednesday June 3, 2020, following the murder of George Floyd and after on-field protests by NFL athletes stirred controversy, an NFL social media employee named Bryndon Minter and a few of his colleagues were upset and decided they needed to do something. Bryndon sent a DM to New Orleans Saints wide receiver Michael Thomas, saying:

> Want to help you create content to be heard around the league. I'm an NFL social media employee and am embarrassed by how the league has been silent this week. The NFL hasn't condemned racism. The NFL hasn't said that Black Lives Matter. I want to help you put the pressure on. And arm you with a video that expresses YOUR voice and what you want from the league. Give me a holler if you want to work together, thanks bro.[10]

Hitting "send," he wasn't sure he would get a response. But Bryndon was sure that hitting that button meant, that, as he was, as he said, "going rogue," since the NFL had no knowledge of what was happening.

In less than an hour, Michael responded, "Hell, yeah! Let's do it!" He also agreed to recruit other NFL players to participate.[11]

Bryndon and his friend Nick Toney set to work that night to write a script and Michael recruited his fellow NFL players Patrick Mahomes, Odell Beckham, Jr., Saquon Barkley, Tyrann Mathieu, DeAndre Hopkins, Deshaun Watson, and Ezekiel Elliott to join in. Videos of the players reading the script poured in and they were compiled into the video that Michael posted to his Twitter account at 9:14 p.m. on Thursday June 4, 2020.

The video began with these words, each line spoken by a different player:

> It's been 10 days since George Floyd was brutally murdered.
> How many times do we need to ask you to listen to your players?
> What will it take?
> For one of us to be brutally murdered?

It segued to DeAndre saying, "I am George Floyd," followed by other players saying successively . . .

> I am Breonna Taylor.
> I am Ahmaud Arbery.
> I am Eric Garner.
> I am Laquan McDonald.
> I am Tamir Rice.
> I am Trayvon Martin.
> I am Walter Scott.
> I am Michael Brown, Jr.
> I am Samuel Dubose.
> I am Frank Smart.
> I am Phillip White.
> I am Jordan Baker.

The video closed with the players demanding . . .

On behalf of the National Football League, this is what
we, the players, would like to hear you state: We, the National Football League, condemn racism and the sys-
tematic oppression of black people. We, the National
Football League, admit wrong in silencing our players
from peacefully protesting. We, the National Football
League, believe black lives matter.[12]

A firestorm of responses lit up social media, spreading
virally around the world. Bryndon wasn't fired for his unsanc-
tioned action, he was in fact praised by the NFL's spokesman,
Brian McCarthy. And on the evening of Friday, June 5, Roger
Goodell posted a video from his basement (since COVID lockdowns were raging) saying verbatim what the players had
asked for.[13]

Less than a month later, the NFL announced it had launched
a social justice endeavor, Inspire Change, promising $250 million
in funding over ten years, to be focused on four areas: education, economic advancement, police and community relations,
and criminal justice reform. The players won through the story
they told.

NEVER FEAR RAISING UNCOMFORTABLE FACTS

While people wish to be settled, it's the job of leaders to be professional unsettlers.[14] We make a habit of telling stories of those we serve,
and while sometimes these stories are uncomfortable and disquieting
for our team to hear, they must nonetheless be told.

Seventy-five percent of my NFL players today are Black men. The
NFLPA funds research through a detailed and rigorous request for
proposal (RFP) process designed and administered by my NFLPA
partner Sean Sansiveri. After a thorough review of the proposals submitted from a variety of academic institutions for our Whole Player,
Whole Life, Whole Family initiative—both internally and with

commissioned outside experts—Harvard University was chosen, not the least because they took the initiative very seriously and comprehensively. Thus began the Football Players Health Study at Harvard (FPHSH), which includes among many other research efforts, a survey of former NFL players. To date, this survey has amassed data from more than 4,000 men who played the game.

The results of the survey continue to evolve, but one insight is particularly powerful and devastating. Of the five negative health outcomes studied (physical function, cognitive function, pain, depression, and anxiety), all five were significantly worse in Black players than they were in White players. The study explained, in typically dry scientific language, "Social and economic advantages of playing professional football did not appear to equalize race disparities in health."[15]

Put perhaps more colorfully by my friend Dr. Herman Taylor, the glories and financial successes of playing in the NFL do not inoculate players against the horrific toll of racial health disparities. As Dr. Martin Luther King, Jr., said, "Of all the racial disparities, surely the disparities in health are the most serious and unjust."[16]

Just as Bryndon Minter and Michael Thomas teamed up to address social justice inequities, we will continue to advocate for tearing down racial health inequities, as we must. While it may be uncomfortable for those in authority to hear the tragic story that their players' lives are still negatively affected by playing professional football, that "professional unsettling" must be done. (And perhaps that's why certain of my colleagues with the NFL have referred to me as a "pro-inflammatory cytokine," which is a biochemical signal to upregulate inflammation . . .)

OPEN YOUR HEART AND TRUST THE STORY

While storytelling is an awesome responsibility, it is important to be forgiving of yourself and others when telling stories. Sometimes, despite the best efforts and intentions, it doesn't quite come out the way we intended.

As the medical director for Fairfax County Police Helicopter and Special Weapons and Tactics units, I had responsibility for medical direction of their operations. On a crisp winter day, January 25, 1993, a Pakistani national pulled his car to the side of the road just outside the entrance to CIA headquarters at the George Bush Center for Intelligence in Langley, Virginia. Hoisting a semiautomatic rifle, he walked among a line of cars waiting to make a left turn into the CIA complex, opening fire and killing two men and injuring three others, before getting back in his car, fleeing the scene, and returning to Pakistan.

One of the injured men, Nicholas Starr, had been shot in the upper arm, nearly amputating it. It remained attached to his body by only the smallest amount of tissue. He lost a massive amount of blood before my police helicopter medics, Ray Tricarico and Kenny Brennan, arrived on scene and urgently medevaced him to Inova Fairfax Hospital's trauma center, where I was chair of emergency medicine. The trauma team, led by Dr. Art Trask, chief of trauma surgery, and me, stabilized Nicholas with tourniquets and gave him 28 units of O-negative blood—a massive transfusion, nearly three times his entire blood volume—before he was stable enough to go to surgery.

The hospital CEO instructed me that I would be the designated spokesman to the media, who crowded around the helipad for interviews. Because of the huge amount of blood it took to save Mr. Starr's life, an urgent call had gone out for blood donors, since 28 units seriously depleted our supply. After many questions during the live news conference, I heard the national reporter from CBS ask me, "What blood type is Mr. Starr?"

While I didn't panic, I did gulp audibly, before hearing myself say, "I don't know what blood type he was before, but he's O-negative now!" I thought that was about the biggest boneheaded move in my career, but the reporters all laughed. Fifteen minutes later the Fairfax County Police Chief, Colonel Mike Young, called me and I thought, "Oh no, he's not going to be happy about that one!"

But the first words out of his mouth were, "Doc, that is the funniest thing I have ever heard a real person say."

When telling a story, open your heart and you will know what to say. Even if it's "He's O-negative now!" (And it doesn't hurt if the story has a self-deprecating tone . . .)

KNOW THE STORY BEFORE YOU TELL THE STORY

Know the message you are conveying with precision and clarity. Anyone who has faced reporters asking questions has learned what former secretary of state Henry Kissinger said when facing a sea of reporters at a press conference after a major summit. His opening line was:

Do any of you have questions for my answers?[17]

Know your message, know your story, and stick to it. The great running back and special teams player for the Washington Redskins, Brian Mitchell, taught me that lesson when he told me:

Doc, sometimes folks will ask you a question that doesn't have good intent—they want you to spill some dirt. I've learned to give them a long answer, telling them in detail what I wanted to say, not the question they asked. Later when they listen to their tape recorder, they realize, "Dang, he didn't answer my question!"[18]

TELL HEROIC STORIES

I finish this chapter with a story about the heroes we were honored to serve in Ukraine . . . showing who the real heroes are.

During the month of April 2022—soon after the war with Russia broke out—I had the privilege of leading a Mobile Emergency Team to Ukraine, supported by the NFL Players Association and organized and supported logistically by Team Rubicon. Upon returning, I was swarmed by reporters who asked, "Dr. Mayer, you are a hero, you chose to go into harm's way during a war to care for the Ukrainian people! What was that like?" I quickly told them, "I'm no hero. But let me tell you about the 350 Ukrainian people whom we had the privilege of treating. They are the heroes. Their bravery, courage, and tenacity make *them* the heroes!"

Anyone not deeply and forever moved by those brave and tenacious people would be unworthy of calling themselves a part of the healing professions. These patients had been ripped out of their lives, often witnessing the destruction of their homes, forced to bring only whatever was most precious to them and moving 900 miles to the West. What would you bring? Can you even imagine having to make such heart-rending choices? We can't—and we saw it in those 350 people, as they left behind the lives they had spent decades building. What would you bring? What would you leave behind?

I can say with certainty what they did not leave behind . . . their dignity, their courage, their commitment to stand firm for Ukraine and rebuild—someday, somewhere—their own lives and futures. They were, without exception, straight-backed, resolute, and deeply grateful for the care given them. Here are just a few of their stories.

- At a train station (a particularly demonic target for Russian missiles), we saw a nine-year-old-boy with an acute respiratory infection. In Ukraine, you'll often hear the saying "Slava Ukraini!" meaning "Glory to Ukraine." After saying this to him, he shouted, proudly, "Heroiam Slava!" or "Glory to the Heroes!" Then he said something that made the interpreter begin to weep. "What did he say?" I asked. The interpreter turned to me and said, "He said, 'Tell the American doctor not to worry about the Ukrainian people. We will be fine!'" What this child brought was unalloyed courage . . .

- At a Catholic retreat, a 73-year-old lady of great dignity came with complaints of hypertension, anxiety, and mild heart failure. She chose to bring her husband, who had just had a lacunar stroke (with the common, yet satanic side effect of violent mood swings), as well as another cherished possession—her cocoa toy chihuahua, Tyson. While we treated her physical ailments and later climbed five flights of stairs to evaluate her husband, I intuitively knew her spirit was most in need of care, and I needed to make her laugh in the midst of her tragedy. So, I placed my stethoscope on Tyson's tiny head and told her, through our interpreter, "Looks like this guy needs some psychotherapy!" Which fortunately had the desired effect—the lady couldn't help but laugh. What she brought was her ability to laugh and retain hope, even in a crisis . . .

- During one of the incessant air raids, our patients came with us to the bomb shelter so we could continue evaluating and treating them in that eerily backlit setting. A 10-year-old girl had injured her knee while escaping from Donetsk and needed a brace and anti-inflammatory medication. But she also needed to talk. As the sirens blared above us, Liane, our nurse from Duke, taught her to take vital signs and I had her listen to her own heart, then mine, after which she declared she wanted to be a doctor "When this is all over." She also said what she missed most was playing basketball. With her mother's permission, we sent her picture to the dean of the School of Medicine at Duke, as well as the women's basket-ball coach, asking them to be ready for a superstar in a few years. We helped her knee a little, but her spirit a lot. What she brought were her undimmed hopes and dreams . . .

- In a Catholic church converted to a shelter for internally displaced persons (a horribly sterile term for these rich lives . . .), we saw a proud woman of 87 who spoke French as well as Ukrainian. She had multiple medical problems and was so taken with our team that she kept cheerfully getting back in line to have us evaluate yet another concern. After helping her climb five floors to the housing area, her 35-year-old son returned to ask me, "Please help me. I don't know what to do, but I think you will know. Should I stay and take care of my mother or join the army?" What would you say? I simply told him that his mother was a kind and brave person, and that people would undoubtedly take good care of her. But I also told him that while there are thousands of men volunteering to serve Ukraine, his mother only had one son. What he brought was his love for his mother . . . and his country.

I wish you could have met the 350 souls for whom we did "house calls" and witness the kindness in their eyes, the wisdom in their smiles, and their steely resolve to persevere as they told us the stories of their lives in unimaginable circumstances.

When you hear of these millions of such displaced people in Ukraine, torn from their lives when they should have been enjoying their homes, going to work and school, and socializing with family and friends, please take a moment to reflect that each of them have stories to tell that deserve to be heard and dreams that deserve to be fulfilled. All of them need our support and will for decades to come.

Many people have shown their kindness by opening their hearts and their pocketbooks—we had the great honor of opening our passports and being welcomed into Ukraine to care for these brave and resilient people. I hope you won't forget them. I know I never will.

What would you bring?[19]

Bring the right words to tell the right story about the right heroes . . .

Now let's turn to how stories can drive questions, not answers . . .

THE HEALING POWER OF THE STORY SUMMARY

- But the right story is priceless . . .
- Don't just write words, sentences, paragraphs or chapters . . . write stories.
- The story should always be about the people you serve and the teams leading them.
- Become the Chief Story Teller.
- Open your heart and you'll know what to say.

9

ASK THE MORE BEAUTIFUL QUESTION

always the more beautiful answer who asks the more beautiful question

EE CUMMINGS[1]

In 2004, as I was standing on the sidelines watching an NFL game with Gene Upshaw and Dr. Elliot Pellman, then the NFL medical advisor, a player went down hard after a tackle and was slow to get up. For some reason, a thought went through my mind and I voiced it out loud, "If that player had a cervical spine injury, who would be responsible for intubating his airway?" That is, who would put a breathing tube down his trachea on the field?

Elliott pointed to the end zone and said, "They would," pointing to the paramedics stationed at the end of the field.

Placing a breathing tube into a massive man on an NFL field with 80,000 fans in the stands and millions more on TV, all watching intently, would require the utmost skill. Skill at this level would be born from extensive experience for the best of emergency physicians, let alone a paramedic, who does far fewer of them in a lifetime of experience.

I told Gene and Elliott, "We have to fix that immediately. It's a matter of 'when,' not 'if' a cardiac arrest will occur on an NFL field."

That was the genesis of the NFL-NFLPA Emergency Action Plans (EAPs), requiring that a cascade of highly qualified emergency personnel be present on the sidelines of every NFL game. Those plans must be submitted to me for approval and practiced in detail twice each year.

Fast forward to the brisk night of January 2, 2023, in the 1st quarter of the game between the Buffalo Bills and the Cincinnati Bengals. Damar Hamlin, the free safety for the Bills, made what appeared to be a routine tackle of the Bengals wide receiver, with both of them falling to the ground. After a brief pause, Damar jumped up but instantly fell back to the turf. As the Bills' medical staff and the sideline emergency personnel responded, it was quickly apparent that he had suffered a cardiac arrest.

Responding precisely according to the EAP, the team, led by Dr. Woods Curry, the code leader and airway management physician, swung into action expertly and rapidly converting Damar from cardiac arrest to a normal heartbeat. Following a course of expert treatment from some of the world's best resuscitation scientists, including Drs. Jason McMullan, Bret Betz, William Knight IV, and Tim Pritts, he was discharged five days later, neurologically and functionally intact in every way.

On April 18, following his recovery and a long process of evaluation, the Buffalo Bills' medical team cleared him for his return to football. Damar stated, "This is not the end of my story."[2]

Beautiful questions can save lives . . .

WHY ASK WHY?

Every parent has had the experience of taking a long car ride with their four-year-old child, who incessantly peppers them with a succession of "Whys."

- Daddy, why do I have to sit in the back?
- Mommy, why do we have to breathe?

- Why is broccoli good if it tastes so bad?
- Why is candy bad if it tastes so good?
- Why is my friend mean to me if she's my friend?

And my personal favorite:

- Why is the sky blue?

Instead of creating awe, amazement, and wonder as they should, these whys from our kids instead irritate us. We conveniently forget that all of us were at one time that four-year-old. While there are many reasons for that (we would prefer to listen to music, think about how crappy the day was at work, or even worse why we hate our jobs so much . . .), I think the main reason is that we falsely believe that we think we are *expected to know the answers*. Why? Because we're the parent and parents are supposed to know everything, aren't we? (Substitute boss, supervisor, team leader, coach, teacher for the other aspects of the "whys" in your life . . .) That is hogwash and the absolute height of arrogance and hubris. The good news is that there is a better way:

We're not supposed to know the right answers
to all the questions.
But we should expect to know how to ask the right questions.

Instead of basking in the false notion that satisfaction derives from answers, we must understand that satisfaction in fact resides in the questions. As Wiesel says, "Answers? I say there are none."[3] Rilke captures this perfectly in his wonderful *Letters to a Young Poet*, a terse tract that is essential reading for those who lead.

> Be patient toward all that is unsolved in your heart and try to love the questions themselves, like locked rooms and like books that are now written in a very foreign tongue. Do not now seek the answers, which cannot be given you because you would not be able to live them. And the point is, to live everything. Live the questions now. Perhaps you will then gradually, without noticing it, live along some distant day into the answer.[4]

There is so much that is unsolved in our hearts that trying to "love the questions themselves—leads us develop the habits of asking questions, not formulating elegant answers. That starts with trust.

This simple equation never fails:

$$No\ trust = No\ questions = No\ innovations$$

Our four-year-olds (and our previous four-year-old selves) ask the questions because they *trust* you, at least until we snap at them, "Because, just because . . ." When they lapse into sullen silence, we wonder why.

Instead, consider a different approach, "You know, that's a great question—thanks for asking that question. I don't know why but I'll bet we can find out together when we get home." Or "Maybe the sky is blue because it makes us happy. Are you happy when the sky is blue?"

How can we discover, as ee cummings said, "the more beautiful question?" The key to asking the right or more beautiful question is to ask a lot of questions—as Rilke said, "love the questions themselves."

My wife Maureen and I raised three wonderful boys, now young men. But when they were young, if I observed them doing something they shouldn't be doing, I would ask, after sniffing the air:

What's that smell? Why, I think it's your immortal soul,
burning in Hell.

If our answer to "Why?" is "Because, just because . . ." perhaps we should sniff the air and wonder what that smell is . . . (Perhaps as bad as when we are questioned as to why we are doing the "Stupid Stuff" and we answer, "*Because we've <u>always</u> done it that way . . .*" I know what that smell is . . .)

THE SOCRATIC METHOD

There is a reason that the Socratic method has stood the test of time over the centuries, dating as it does from the fifth century BCE. Plato first described this approach in *Theaetetus*, comprising as it does the central concept of a cooperative, yet argumentative dialogue between individuals. This dialogue is based on a series of difficult yet essential questions being asked and answered, only to lead to even more fundamental questions, particularly about underlying assumptions.[5]

It is also known as *elenchus*, which is the discipline of applying Socratic principles in a penetrating fashion. While highly effective in distilling reasoning, the Socratic method is not inherently easy because it requires discipline.

Ward Farnsworth wrote a superb book titled *The Socratic Method: A Practitioner's Handbook*, in which he notes, "Socrates didn't question people in order to teach us how to question people. He did it to teach us *how to think*."[6] Based on the way most of us have been raised and educated, we default to what in theology and logic is known as "the argument from authority," based on blindly accepting certain things as essential, almost universal verities. Like Peer Gynt peeling an onion,[7] Socrates teaches us how to use questions to peel back the layers of assumptions to get to the essential core within, giving us a stronger foundation and the wisdom underlying it.

Nonetheless, the constant questioning of the Socratic method, like the questions of the four-year-old, can be . . . well, frankly, irritating after a while. (And let's recall that these questions finally resulted in Socrates being tried and sentenced to death by drinking poison . . . just sayin' . . .) That irritation is part of what Ralph Waldo Emerson meant when he said, "People wish to be settled, but it is only in so far as they are unsettled is there any hope for them."[8] Questions are "unsettlers" and we are the better for them.

LIVE THE QUESTIONS NOW

Questions are still the key, as they were in Socrates' day. Centuries later, Rilke reminds us:

> *And the point is, to live everything. Live the questions now.*

"Living the questions now" is diametrically opposed to accepting answers without the foundation of the questions. I suggest that much of the deep divisions in our society stem from our false sense of certainty not only that *we know*, but conversely that *others don't*. With that mindset, and without living the questions through the discipline of the Socratic method, we are standing on the false foundations of certitudes, which too often breeds contempt for those who refuse to share those certitudes.

As the great writer and philosopher Stephen Frye noted during the Munk Debates in Toronto, May 18, 2018,

> *It is a time not to be too certain. It is a time for engaging,*
> *emotionally fulfilling, passionate, and positive doubt.*[9]

Commitment to doubt starts not by talking, but by listening—isn't that what questions comprise, an opportunity to listen carefully and astutely, in a disciplined, informed way? But we seem more passionate about talking than about listening, about certainty than doubt.

Most of us simply aren't that good at embracing and nurturing silence. We are very good at demanding that others should be silent, sometimes drowning them out so they can't be heard over our shouts. But we are not nearly as good at simply being quiet and engaging in

THE DISCIPLINE OF SILENCE
Silence Is Golden
I asked you previously to take a moment to look at the following six letters, then rearrange them in a way that would provide you with a deeper meaning.

Remember?

LISTEN

As you may recall, the answer is . . .

SILENT

the *active process of silence* to let others speak. (Most people don't really listen anyway, they wait, horribly impatiently, for another chance to talk . . .)

How do we reconcile the passion of our Deep Joy to serve others by leading with the discipline of the silent listening we should employ? My gentle suggestion is this:

> Advocate the passion of your Deep Joy as if you are right.
> But listen as if you were wrong.

While that is another dynamic tension between seemingly contradictory ideas, I have found that it has helped me through the years to lead better by decreasing my certainty, while increasing my passionate and positive doubt.

Innovation and exploration require trust that answers are suspect, but questions are priceless. If we lead that way, perhaps gradually, without noticing it, we might, as Rilke suggests, *"live along some distant day into the answer."*

ASK THE MORE BEAUTIFUL QUESTION SUMMARY

- Develop a four-year-old's habit of asking "Why?"
- We're not supposed to know the answers to all the questions, but . . .
- We are supposed to know how to help others ask all the questions.
- The key to asking more beautiful questions is to ask a *lot* of questions.
- This is a time not for certainty, but for passionate doubt.

10

CAPTURE DATA . . . BUT TREASURE WISDOM

The saddest aspect of life right now is that science gathers knowledge faster than society gathers wisdom.

ISAAC ASIMOV[1]

My former boss, DeMaurice (De) Smith, the executive director of the NFL Players Association, and I forged a core aspect of our strategy, which is:

We will go anywhere the science takes us . . . but nowhere it doesn't.[2]

This is one of the most important insights of my career in football, since we are reluctantly but inexorably forced to negotiate health and safety issues as if they were revenue splits or contracts, instead of letting the science speak for itself.

First, *data* are, as always, the basis of science, the building blocks from which we construct all health and safety initiatives. Compiling the data in the most meaningful way moves us from the scientific data to some semblance of *knowledge*—what those data might mean. Distilling that knowledge for its meaning leads us to *wisdom*, which is the next step, but not the final step.

The final step is the never-ending one, acting on the knowledge that wisdom constantly moves forward as new data and new knowledge evolves from the science. We are always questioning, always experimenting, never satisfied we have reached our final destination. Indeed, in this fast-changing world, there is no final destination.

As the great poet and philosopher, Robert Frost, noted, wisdom is often a "momentary stay against confusion."[3] It's momentary precisely because it is iterative. Data and knowledge change as fast as science progresses. Wisdom changes more slowly—as it should—but it does change iteratively. (And for those of you are movie buffs, De refers to me as "Keyser Söze," the compelling and relentless character from *The Usual Suspects*[4] . . . perhaps testament to my ferocity in pursuing wisdom for the benefit of our player-patients.)

Data, knowledge, and wisdom are not only *not* the same thing—they are not even *remotely the same thing.* Most folks thought data and knowledge were the Holy Grail, but they have proven False Gods in the search for the wisdom of "how to be" while leading. Data and knowledge are *necessary* conditions—they must be there for success in our journey toward wisdom. But they are not *sufficient* conditions. Even when present they do not guarantee success.

MOORE'S LAW

Even though data and knowledge are doubling at an unheard of rate, indeed unimaginable only a decade ago, the distillation process to extract wisdom from them is essential to help us lead.

Moore's Law, originally described in 1965 by Gordon Moore, cofounder and later CEO of Fairchild Semiconductor, stated that the number of transistors in an integrated circuit doubled every two years.[5] This law was later extended to describe the amount of time it takes to double the world's existing data.

Now data doubles every two years—perhaps even faster than that. How long until it doubles every two days? Every two hours? Every two minutes or seconds?

According to recent statistics . . .

- There are currently around 4.95 billion active internet users around the globe.

- On average in 2020, each person on the face of this earth created an average of 1.7 megabytes of data *every second.*

- About 2.5 exabytes of data were produced *globally* every single day in 2022 (an exabyte is 1 billion gigabytes).

- By 2025, this number is expected to grow to 463 exabytes per day.[6]

We are at least figuratively, and often literally, choking on data, unable to digest the sheer volume of the meal. As Asimov pointed out, wisdom doubles more slowly, and wisely so . . .

This deluge of data simply cannot, even with the most sophisticated of computers, be conflated with either knowledge or wisdom. (For fans of artificial intelligence, the argument is that AI will be able to analyze, at a minimum, the burgeoning sources of data into knowledge and perhaps knowledge into wisdom. While never one to scoff at possibility, the former will likely occur, but I have serious doubts about the latter— knowledge to wisdom. Far more importantly, my friends who are experts in AI have told me not to expect it.)

DEFINITIONS DRIVE SOLUTIONS

Definitions drive solutions, meaning that the very process of defining terms should guide us to action on how to improve and lead most effectively. With that in mind, here are my definitions of data, knowledge, and wisdom.

Data are unstructured information points, which while organized in some fashion by their description, do not independently coalesce into actionable knowledge. Graduation rates at each of the approximately 1,100 NCAA schools by sport is an example of data. But do those data indicate the *quality* of the education? No. And it certainly doesn't give us the *wisdom* to know *what to do with those data.*

Data drives knowledge but not *all* data translates to knowledge, which accounts for the concept of the "signal to noise ratio." The cacophonous noise of the flood of data drowns out the knowledge—the signal—nascent in that data.

Knowledge structures and organizes data so that they can be used strategically, both to find a distillation toward wisdom and to guide future data collection to prove or disprove the issue at hand. The key is to ensure that future knowledge will be an iteration of current knowledge in a progressive way, bolstered by new data as they emerge.

Wisdom, the final and most elusive piece, takes knowledge as structured to fit the strategy and adds the key pieces of how this fits with the Deep Joy of the team and the individual leader, adding values and social context into the equation. The Irish poet William Butler Yeats remarked:

> *There is some one Myth for every man*
> *which, if we but knew it,*
> *would tell us all that he did and all that he thought.*[7]

In the previous example, NCAA graduation rates are the data, hopefully used to assist the knowledge of what the data mean, and the wisdom lies in knowing what to do going forward to best assure that those athletes' lives are positively affected.

That goes far beyond graduation rates and "gold stars" for those teams with the highest rates to important questions such as, "How did being a member of these teams positively impact their lives?" and "What were the costs (physically, mentally, emotionally, psychologically, and spiritually) to enact that benefit?" Finally, "Did the *benefits enacted* from being on a team and graduating from college exceed the *toll extracted* in the process?"

As you can see, the calculus gets infinitely more complex, as do the data, as we move up that chain toward knowledge and wisdom. So, while we may assume that attending and graduating from college as a part of a team is beneficial to the student-athlete, more data and knowledge will likely be needed to scientifically support this assumed wisdom.

And the closer we get to the groundwater of data and knowledge, the more wise our wisdom will become.

There is great wisdom in knowing which data to mine, which are most likely take us from data to knowledge and knowledge to wisdom.

The progressive distillation from data to knowledge and knowledge to wisdom looks like this:

What does it say?   Data
What does it tell us?   Knowledge
What does it mean?   Wisdom

Data, knowledge, and wisdom help us lead by acting as the foundations from which we develop objectives, strategies to attain those objectives, and the wisest tactics to achieve the chosen strategy. It's essential here to keep Sun Tzu's wisdom from *The Art of War* in mind:

Strategy without tactics is the slowest route to victory.
Tactics without strategy is the noise before defeat.[8]

Don't let an excessive focus on data and knowledge bereft of wisdom be "the noise before defeat" . . .

But the wisdom of the great philosopher Mike Tyson is also true:

Everyone has a strategy until they get hit in the mouth.[9]

Sometimes the distillation of wisdom from data and knowledge comes at the high cost of "getting hit in the mouth." But it's always worth it . . .

WISDOM IN INNOVATION

Two of my mentors are Drs. Ralph Snyderman and Sandy Williams, formerly the chancellor of Health Affairs and dean of the School of Medicine (respectively) at my alma mater, Duke University. In 2003, Ralph and Sandy published a paper in the prestigious journal *Science* that was instrumental in advancing the concept of precision, personalized medicine. (The idea was so paradigm shattering that many people now claim to have originated it—proving the dictum that "Good ideas have many parents—bad ideas are illegitimate children.")

But Ralph and Sandy deserve much credit for the innovation.

Like many important innovations, precision medicine is achingly simple—no two people with the same disease react to the disease and its treatment in the same way or to the same extent—even members of the same family. Patients with every disease from hypertension, diabetes, and cardiovascular disease to infectious diseases like COVID-19 react to the disease or its treatments in individual ways. Hence the requirement for precision (specific treatments for each individual) and personalized medicine—designed to meet each person's unique biology and personal needs. To realize this potential, transformational models of prospective healthcare are being created and validated. Prospective healthcare determines the risk for individuals to develop certain diseases, detect the disease's earliest onset, and prevent or intervene early enough to provide maximum benefit. Each individual should have a personalized, precision health plan to accomplish this. No more "one size fits all," reactive approaches to disease will do. Instead, prospective, precision, personalized approaches will guide both the patient and her doctors.

How did Ralph and Sandy arrive at this insight? Both are internal medicine–trained specialists, with Ralph subspecializing in rheumatology and Sandy in cardiology—two seemingly disparate areas. Both were studying genes and proteins that regulate cellular processes of health and disease. They found striking structural and functional variability in these regulatory genes and proteins that underlie the variability of responses among different people. Their thinking resulted in a simple but vital envisioning of the role of medicine moving forward.

Many medical scientists have contributed data and knowledge to the development of precision, personalized medicine. But Ralph and Sandy took the initiative to understand its meaning and massive implications, and to give voice to that their understanding.[10, 11, 12]

The same personalized, precision approach must be taken to leading in times of crisis—no two leaders will face the same crises nor will they lead in the same way—each leader must have their own unique personalized and precision approach, developed iteratively over time through experience, forming and leading an expert team (not just a team of experts), innovating at the speed of trust, making failure their fuel, getting the C-suite and the We-suite together on both the take-off and the landing, sucking down instead of sucking up, focusing on actions, not slogans, telling the story of those we serve, and asking the more beautiful questions—all in service of your Deep Joy. This book is an effort to help you navigate your personalized, precision leading in every walk of life.

Now, having laid the stones of each of the chapters into the riprap of our path through this book, let's next turn to how to put all of this together.

CAPTURE DATA . . . BUT TREASURE WISDOM SUMMARY

- Data, knowledge, and wisdom are not remotely the same thing.
- What does it say? = Data
- What does it tell us? = Knowledge
- What does it mean? = Wisdom

CONCLUSION
FIND YOUR DEEP JOY

Having laid what I hope is a strong foundation for how the lessons I learned leading a life in crisis might be helpful to you, your teams, and your organization, let's turn now to some thoughts on how all of this fits together. I do this to ensure that you get the greatest possible value from the ideas I have presented to you in this book.

The only reason to ever give a speech, have a conversation, or write a book, memo, email, or letter (remember those?) is to help someone, not lecture them. I hope the somewhat contrarian thoughts of this book will help you as you leave "Someday . . ." behind and choose to lead "Today!" By focusing on leading as a verb—something you *do*—and leaving behind leadership as a noun—something you *say*—you begin the process of taking control of your life and of choosing adventure over safety.

Begin leading as a verb by asking the right questions. In my many years of leading in crisis, I have found the most important of these questions to be:

How should I *be today*, leading my life and my team?

What is my *Deep Joy*?

How does *this action*, in *this moment*, reflect that Deep Joy?

What will my legacy be today?

Then, at the close of each day, take a few moments to pause, reflect, and answer these three important questions:

What are three good things that happened today?

What role did I play in creating these three good things?

How will I be tomorrow to lead?

Use each of the chapters in this book, and the insights you have gained from them, as your North Star to direct your adventurous journey—contemplating how the contrarian thoughts can help you lead yourself and inspire others to lead. Remember: You are always being watched by others—how you lead is a model for how those around you will lead. Every minute of every day, you can choose to be a good model, a bad model, or something in between.

I've been immensely fortunate to have lived an interesting life, filled with leading in times of crisis on the world stage. Each one of these experiences has made me a better and more effective leader. And remember: the greatest lessons I've learned about leading were from the many smart and talented people around me. I'm eternally grateful for the lessons they taught me over the years, and I hope the lessons I've learned will be of help to you, your family, and your team.

There's one more thing I want you to always remember:

The leader you are looking for . . . *is you!*

I mentioned earlier that in addition to being a football player, I was a theology major in college. One of the required courses was called Storytelling, which was a full semester's worth of stories that were specifically designed to illustrate the scriptures we had been assigned to study. Although we called it "Hokey Story Time," I must admit that many of those stories have stuck with me in the decades since.

I close this chapter—and this book—with one of the stories from that class that deeply influenced me.

BE A STAR THROWER

You are involved in one of the greatest endeavors one could hope for: leading yourself, your family, and your team in times of crisis. The story I'm about to tell you was inspired by a short essay—"The Star Thrower"—written by the incomparable natural scientist and philosopher Dr. Loren Eiseley.[1]

I should warn you at the outset that this story is probably apocryphal and certainly sentimental, if not outright "hokey." But it is important enough that I will ask your forbearance in my telling it . . .

In the nation's capital area, many people choose to take their summer vacations at the Outer Banks of North Carolina, the barrier islands off the coast, which extend well off the shore into the Atlantic Ocean and are connected by a series of bridges and ferries.

One day, a businessperson took his family to the Outer Banks where the houses are located right on the beach, but are built on top of huge, wood pylons, or stilts, so that when the tides surge and the waves smash against them, the houses won't be torn down by nature's force. The businessperson checked in for the week on a Saturday afternoon—bright and sunny and perfect for a vacation.

That night, however, a massive storm howled in off the Atlantic, with driving rain and waves crashing against the pylons. Yet despite the violence of the storm, it had the odd effect of helping the businessperson sleep very well.

The next morning, as usual, he awoke early, to find the sun rising over the Atlantic Ocean, the sky was crystal clear and the ocean perfectly flat. But the tidal surge of the storm had the curious effect of washing onto the beaches of the Outer Banks what appeared to be every starfish in the sea. In fact, it appeared that starfish had rained down on the beach, covering it as far as he could see in both directions.

As he walked down to the beach, the businessperson looked to the left and to the right and saw only one other human on the beach, to his left, so he walked toward the person. As he got closer, his curiosity was piqued, as the person on the beach repeatedly and rhythmically bent over, paused, and then stood back up.

As the businessperson got even closer, he became even more curious because he realized that the other person on the beach was a young girl, about nine years old, all alone. As he got closer, he could see that she was picking up starfish, one by one, then brushing them off and throwing them back into the ocean.

As he finally reached the young girl, the businessperson said, "Little girl, I couldn't help noticing what you are doing as I walked toward you. As noble as it is, I'm sorry to tell you this, but what you are doing can't possibly make a difference. I've been watching you for the last 15 minutes and you've only been able to clear this one small area about 7 feet around."

He continued, "There are thousands of starfish on this beach and many thousands more we can't see," sweeping his arm to show her. "So, I am sorry to tell you this, but what you are doing can't possibly make any difference . . ."

Looking down at the starfish in her hand, and then back up at the man, the little girl replied, "It does to *this* one" as she threw the starfish back into the waves . . .

Well . . . as I said, it's a hokey story, and no one knows if it really happened. But that's what *you* do, isn't it? Every time you lead yourself, your team, and your family, you make a difference in people's lives—you throw that starfish back into the sea. Why? Because it's what great leaders do. Every minute of every day.

BE A HERO

If you have children, ask them what they want to do with their lives, and, regardless of their age, they will tell you, "I want to make a difference in people's lives." There is a word for those who work hard for others, who strive constantly, not for themselves but for others, often against seemingly impossible odds, all for the good of others . . .

Do you know what the word is?

Hero . . .

Here is my question to you: As you lead your life, regardless of your job description or what you do, do you feel like a hero?

You should . . . because if you are not a hero, who is?

You take care of people who can't, won't, don't, who do not fully understand how to take care of themselves. You take care of people who, through the ravages of time, disease, anguish, alcohol, drugs— and even, tragically, their own families—have lost their dignity, and you give it back to them. You do it with style, grace, decency, and equanimity, and you do it person by person, day by day, week by week, year in, year out. And you don't do it for yourself—you do it for others, selflessly, unselfishly.

So, again, I ask: If you are not a hero, who is?

Please do me a favor. The next time your head hits the pillow, either just before or just after you turn out the light, take a moment to smile and say to yourself: "I am a *hero*—I make a difference in people's lives."

Because you are a hero, and I am very proud to be one of you. Serving *you* by writing this book is my own Deep Joy, and I'm pleased that you've made the decision to make a real difference in the lives of those around you. You've chosen to pick up a starfish off the beach and throw it back into the ocean—making a difference in *its* life. And you do it over and over and over.

Now, as this book comes to a close, I leave you with this parting advice:

Live today—and every day—as a leader . . .
Think, act, and innovate . . .
Begin the work within . . .
Be at peace . . .
Show courage . . .
You are a hero . . .
You make a difference . . .
And that is . . . your Deep Joy . . .

NOTES

INTRODUCTION

1. Verstegen M. Remarks to the NFL Players Association Board of Player Representatives Meeting, March 9, 2023, Maui.
2. Leonard E. *New York Times.* July 16, 2001. http://www.nytimes.com/2001/07/16/arts/writers-writing-easy-adverbs-exclamation-points-especially-hooptedoodle.html.
3. Twain M. *The Art of Storytelling,* In: Neider C, ed. *The Complete Essays of Mark Twain.* 1963; Garden City, NY: Doubleday.

CHAPTER 1

1. Kierkegaard S. *Either/Or: A Fragment of Life.* 1992; London: Penguin.
2. Hesselbein F. *My Life in Leadership: The Joys and Lessons Learned Along the Way.* 2011; San Francisco: Jossey-Bass.
3. Sullenberger C. Personal conversation with the author, June 22, 2022, Teton Village, Wyoming.
4. Marshall GC. Quoted in: Morrow L. George C. Marshall: the last great American? *Smithsonian Magazine* 1997; 28 (5): 104–119. https://www.smithsonianmag.com/history/george-c-marshall-the-last-great-american-51100180/. Accessed May 19, 2023.
5. Aristotle. *Nichomachean Ethics.* Bartlett RC, Collins SD, trans. 2022; Chicago: University of Chicago Press.
6. Thomas J. Personal interview with the author, February 24, 2023.
7. Mahomes P. Personal conversation with the author.
8. Batalden P. Speech to Dartmouth College. Institute for Healthcare Improvement, 2015. https://www.ihi.org/communities/blogs/origin-of-every-system-isperfectly-designed-quote. Accessed May 22, 2023.

9. Gretzky W. Quoted in an interview with Bob McKenzie, *The Hockey News*, 1983.

10. Sun Tzu. *The Art of War*. Sawyer RD, trans. 1994; New York: Basic Books.

CHAPTER 2

1. Njoku K. *Book of African Proverbs and Meanings*. 2023; New York: The Rockefeller Society.

2. Tolstoy L. *Anna Karenina*. 2014; Oxford, UK: Oxford University Press.

3. Waldinger R, Schulz M. *The Good Life: Lessons from the World's Longest Scientific Study of Happiness*. 2023; New York: Simon and Schuster.

4. Einstein A. *Zanesville Times Recorder*. June 22, 1972.

5. Belichick B, Quoted in: Brady T, Davis D. Personal conversations with the author, December 10, 2022.]

6. Ensor P. *The Functional Silo Syndrome*. http://www.ame.org/sites/default/files/target_articles/88q1a3.pdf. Accessed April 30, 2020.

7. Lewis CS. *Mere Christianity*. 1952; New York: Harper One.

8. Beaton A. The doctor and the 'badasses' keeping NFL players safe from the coronavirus. *Wall Street Journal*. May 27, 2020. https://www.wsj.com/articles/the-doctor-and-the-badasses-keeping-nfl-players-safe-from-the-coronavirus-11590580800. Accessed June 1, 2023.

9. Mayer T, Cates RJ. *Leadership for Great Customer Service: Satisfied Employees, Satisfied Patients*. 2010; Chicago: Health Administration Press.

10. Klotz A. Quoted in: Cohen A. How to quit your job in the great postpandemic resignation boom. *Bloomberg Business Week*. May 10, 2021. https://www.bloomberg.com/news/articles/2021-05-10/quit-your-job-how-to-resign-after-covid-pandemic#xj4y7vzkg. Accessed May 15, 2023.

11. Gandhi M. *An Autobiography: The Story of My Experiments with Truth*. 1948; Washington, DC: Public Affairs Press.

12. Shakespeare W. *Henry V*. 1995; New York: Simon and Schuster Paperback.

13. Brady T, Guerrero A. Personal conversation with the author, May 4, 2019.

14. Archimedes. Quoted in: Pappas of Alexandria, *Synagoge*, Book VIII.

15. Mahon D. "Everything will be alright." In: Kavanaugh P, ed. *New and Selected Poems*. 2014; Manchester, UK: Carcanet.

16. Mayer T, Strauss R, Tavernero T, et al. The disciplines of teams and teamwork. In: Strauss R, Mayer T, eds. *Strauss and Mayer's Emergency Department Management*. 2021; Dallas: American College of Emergency Physicians Press.

CHAPTER 3

1. Beckett S. *Worstward Ho*. 1980; New York: Grove Press.

2. Mayer T. *Battling Healthcare Burnout: Learning to Love the Job You Have While Creating the Job You Love*. 2021; San Francisco: Berrett-Kohler.

3. Peters T. *Excellence Now: Extreme Humanism*. 2021; Boston: Networlding Publishing.

4. Brim B. Strengths-based leadership: The 4 things followers need. Gallup. October 7, 2021. https://gallup.com/cliftonstrengths/en/251003/strengths-based -leadership-things-followers need.aspx.

5. Brown RM. *Sudden Death*. 1983; New York: Bantam.

6. Kuhn T. *The Structure of Scientific Revolutions: 50th Anniversary Edition*. 2012; Chicago: University of Chicago Press.

7. Bohr N. Quoted in: Dyson FJ. Innovations in physics. *Scientific American* 1958; 199: 74–99.

8. Mayer T, Jensen K. *Hardwiring Flow: Systems and Processes for Seamless Patient Care*. 2010; Gulf Breeze, FL: Fire Starter Press.

9. Csikszentmihalyi M. *Flow: The Psychology of Optimal Experience.*1990; New York: Harper and Row.

10. McKay J. Quoted in: Vuic J. *The Yucks! Two Years in Tampa with the Losingest Team in NFL History*. 2016; New York: Simon and Schuster, p. 196.

11. Maslow A. *Motivation and Personality.*1954; New York: Harper and Row.

12. Nietzsche F. *Beyond Good and Evil*. 2008; New York: Soho Press.

13. Sinek S. *Start with Why: How Great Leaders Inspire Everyone to Take Action*. 2009; New York: Penguin Group.

14. Mayer T. In an interview with Pamela Brown, CNN anchor, May 4, 2022. https://www.youtube.com/watch?v=d74rzdfMEH8. Accessed May 19, 2023.

15. Maslach C, Leiter MP. *The Burnout Challenge: Managing People's Relationships with their Jobs*. 2022; Cambridge, MA: Harvard University Press.

16. Petrino R, Riesego L, Yilmaz B. Burnout in emergency medicine professionals after 2 years of the COVID-19 pandemic: a threat to the healthcare system? *Eur J Emerg Med* 2022; 29 (4): 279–284. doi: 10.1097/ MEJ.0000000000000952. Accessed May 22, 2023.

17. Future Forum Pulse. Executives feel the strain of leading in the "new normal." October 2022. https://futureforum.com/research/pulse-report-fall-2022 -executives-feel-strain-leading-in-new-normal/.

18. Mayer T. *Battling Healthcare Burnout: Learning to Love the Job You Have While Creating the Job you Love*. 2021; Oakland, CA: Berrett-Koehler.

19. Davis D. Personal conversation with the author, October 12, 2023.

20. James H. Quoted in: Edel L. *Henry James: The Master: 1901–1916*, Book Two: *The Beast in the Jungle*, Chapter: Billy, p. 124. 1978; New York: A Discus Book: Avon Books.

CHAPTER 4

1. Edison TA. Edison Innovation Foundation. http://www.thomasedison.org /edison-quotes. Accessed May 7, 2023.

2. Mandela N. In: *Mandela: From Prison to President*, April 26, 1994, documentary short film by Lindsay R. http://www. https://www.imdb.com/title /tt6369882/. Accessed May 7, 2023.

3. Madden J. CBS Sports football broadcast, August 18, 1993.

4. Brady T, Personal conversation with the author, February 2, 2021.

5. Krzyzewski M. Personal conversation with the author, May 19, 2023, Duke University, Feagin Leadership Institute.

6. Twain M. *Pudd'nhead Wilson*. 1894; Chapter 15. 2007; New York: Signet

7. Ecclesiastes 9:11. 2011; New York: Zondervan/HarperCollins.

8. Churchill WS. In a speech to the House of Commons, November 2, 1952. https://hansard.millbanksystems.com/commons/1952/nov/04/debate-on -the-address#S5CV0507P0_19521104_HOC_60. Accessed May 7, 2023.

9. Wambach A. *Wolfpack: How to Come Together, Unleash Our power, and Change the Game*. 2018; New York: Celadon Books.

10. Kipling R. "If." In: *Kipling: Poems*. 2007; New York: Alfred Knopf.

11. Lawson K. Personal conversation with the author, May 20, 2023, Duke University, Feagin Leadership Institute.

12. Smith J. Personal conversation with the author, March 28, 2023, Cape Girardeau, MO.

13. Mandela N. *Long Walk to Freedom: The Autobiography of Nelson Mandela*. 1994; Boston: Little Brown.

14. Brown B. *Dare to Lead: Brave Work. Tough Conversations. Whole Hearts.* 2018; New York: Random House.

15. Kyes J. Quoted in: Mayer T, Cates RJ. *Leadership for Great Customer Service: Satisfied Employees, Satisfied Patients*. 2014; Chicago: Health Administration Press.

16. Seligman ME, Csikszentmihalyi M. Positive psychology: an introduction. *Am Psychol* 2000; 55 (1): 5–14. doi: 10.1037//0003-066x.55.1.5.

17. Han G, Ceilley R. Chronic wound healing: a review of current management and treatment. *Adv Ther* 2017; 34 (3): 599–610. doi: 10.1007/s12325-017-0478-y. Accessed May 22, 2023.

18. Danowski J. Personal interview with the author, June 6, 2007.

19. Mandela N. *Long Walk to Freedom. The Autobiography of Nelson Mandela.* 1994; Boston: Little Brown.

20. Bascomb N. *The Perfect Mile: Three Athletes, One Goal, and Less than Four Minutes to Achieve It.* 2004; Boston: Houghton Mifflin.

21. Fairbank R. Personal conversations with the author, 2019–2022; Morris N. Personal conversations with the author, 2019–2022.

22. Chesterton GK. The eternal revolution. In: *Orthodoxy.* 1908; San Francisco: Ignatius Press.

CHAPTER 5

1. Krzyzewski M. *Leading with the Heart: Coach K's Successful Strategies for Basketball, Business, and Life.* 2000; New York: Grand Central.

2. Smith D. Speech to the NFL Players Association Board of Player Representatives, March 9, 2009, Maui.

3. Kessler J. Personal communication with the author, March 9, 2023.

4. Creasey T. Understanding why people resist change. Prosci. N.d. https://www.prosci.com/blog/understanding-why-people-resist-change. Accessed May 23, 2023.

5. Nimitz-Class-Aircraft Carrier. Naval technology. January 6, 2020. https://www.naval-technology.com/projects/nimitz/. Accessed May 23, 2023.

6. Starling, Denby, Admiral. Conversation with the author aboard the USS George Washington at sea, April 10, 2010.

7. Tretter JC. Why the NFL's approach to field surfaces is uneven. April 19, 2023. https://nflpa.com/posts/nfl-approach-field-surface-uneven. Accessed May 7, 2023.

8. Blanchard K. Sharing Information About Yourself. https://www.linkedin.com/pulse/sharing-information-yourself-ken-blanchard/, accessed November 15, 2023.

9. Churchill WS. Quoted in: Gilbert M. *Churchill's War Leadership.* 2004; New York: Random House.

10. Cusick P. Personal communication with the author, April 27, 2023.

CHAPTER 6

1. Goldsmith M. All of us are stuck on suck ups. 2003. Fast Company, December 1, 2003, p. 117.

2. Shakespeare W. *Henry V.* 1995; New York: Simon and Schuster Paperback.

3. Greenleaf R. *Servant Leadership: A Journey into the Nature of Legitimate Power and Greatness.* 2002; New York: Paulist Press.

4. Osler W. *Aequanimitus.* 1904; Philadelphia: HK Lewis Publishers.

5. Groopman J. *How Doctors Think*. 2007; Boston: Houghton Mifflin.

6. Centers for Disease Control, Health Alert Update, October 18, 2001, 1:27 PM EDT. Recommendations for visitors or employees who were in the Hart Senate Office Building on 10/15/01. https://stacks.cdc.gov/view/cdc/24949. Accessed May 17, 2023.

7. Meir G. Quoted in: Shenker I, Shenker M, eds. *As Good as Golda: The Warmth and Wisdom of Israel's Prime Minister by Golda Meir*. 1970; New York: The McCall Publishing Company.

8. Bohr N. Quoted in: Heisenberg W. *Physics and Beyond: Encounters and Conversations*. Pomerans AJ, trans., Chapter 8, Atomic Physics and Pragmatism, p. 102. 1971; New York: Harper and Row.

9. Frankl V. *Man's Search for Meaning*. 1992; Boston: Beacon Press.

10. Somervell B. Quoted in: Morrow L. George C. Marshall: the last great American? *Smithsonian Magazine* 1997; 28 (5): 104–119. https://www.smithsonianmag.com/history/george-c-marshall-the-last-great-american-51100180/. Accessed May 19, 2023.

11. Mayer J. Personal conversation with the author, May 22, 2005.

CHAPTER 7

1. Emerson RW. *Letters and Social Aims*. 1894; Boston: Houghton Mifflin.

2. Mayer T, Cates RJ. *Leadership for Great Customer Service: Satisfied Employees, Satisfied Customers*. 2014; Chicago: Health Administration Press.

3. https://movieposters.ha.com/itm/movie-posters/miscellaneous/facebook-motivational-posters-facebook-2010s-screen-print-posters-4-16-x-20-total-4-items-/a/7132-86472.s

4. Brooks M. *History of the World, Part 1*. https://youtu.be/PmZFGw5CeWE. Accessed May 22, 2023.

5. Mayer T. Putting it all together: best practices in service excellence. *Healthcare Executive*. January–February 2011.

6. Danowski J. Interview at Koskinen Stadium, Duke University, May 13, 2023.

CHAPTER 8

1. Von Blixen K (nee Isak Dinesen). In an interview with Mohn B. *New York Times Book Review*. November 3, 1957.

2. Twain M, William Dean Howells. In: Neider C, ed. *The Complete Essays of Mark Twain*. 1963; Garden City, NY: Doubleday, pp. 400–401.

3. Auden WH. Musee des beaux arts. *New Writing*, Spring 1939.

4. Twain M. *Letters from the Earth: Uncensored Writings*. DeVoto B, ed. 1962; New York: Harper and Row.

5. Twain M. Quoted in: Bainton G, ed. *The Art of Authorship, Reminiscences, Methods of Work, and Advice to Young Beginners.* 1890; New York: Appleton and Company, p. 87.

6. Njoku K. *Book of African Proverbs and Meanings.* 2023; New York: The Rockefeller Society.

7. Wiesel E. *Legends of Our Time.* 2004; New York: Schocken Books.

8. Alighieri D. *The Inferno.* Ciardi J, trans. 2016; New York: New American Library.

9. Buber M. *Tales of the Hasidim.* 1994; New York: Schocken Books.

10. Minter B. Personal interview with the author, April 24, 2023.

11. Thomas M. Personal interview with the author, May 7, 2023.

12. Thomas M. https://twitter.com/Cantguardmike/status/126871274386092 8513. Accessed May 22, 2023.

13. Goodell R. https://www.espn.com/video/clip/_/id/29272773. Accessed May 19, 2023.

14. Emerson RW. *Essays and Lectures.* 1983; New York: Library of America.

15. Roberts AL, Taylor HA, Whittington AJ et al. Race in association with physical and mental health among former American-style football players: Findings of the Football Players Health Study at Harvard. *Annals of Epidemiology* 2020; 51: 48–52.

16. King ML. In a press conference March 25, 1966, prior to a speech at the Medical Committee for Human Rights, Chicago.

17. Kissinger H. Opening remarks to a press conference as US Secretary of State, November 6, 1976.

18. Mitchell B. Personal conversation with the author.

19. Mayer T. What would you bring? https://nflpa.com/posts/what-would-you -bring. Accessed May 22, 2023.

CHAPTER 9

1. Cummings ee. *Introduction: Collected Poems.* 1938; New York: Harcourt Brace.

2. Hamlin D. Press conference announcing his return to the NFL, April 18, 2023. https://www.buffalobills.com/video/damar-hamlin-speaks-for-the -first-time-since-cardiac-event-not-the-end-of-my-sto. Accessed May 19, 2023.

3. Wiesel E. *Legends of Our Time.* 1968; New York: Schocken.

4. Rilke RM. *Letters to a Young Poet.* 2013; New York: Penguin Classics..

5. Plato. *Theaetetus.* 1992; London: Hackett Classics.

6. Farnsworth W. *The Socratic Method: A Practitioner's Guide.* 2021; Boston: Godine.

7. Ibsen H. *Peer Gynt.* 2017; New York: Penguin Classics.

8. Emerson RW. *Letters and Social Aims.* 1894; Boston: Houghton Mifflin.

9. Frye S. Munk Debates, May 18, 2018. https://www.youtube.com/watch?v=LJKXJNM3W-c. Accessed May9, 2023.

CHAPTER 10

1. Asimov I, Shulman J. *Isaac Asimov's Book of Nature and Science Quotations.* 1988; New York: Grove.

2. Mayer T. Quote of the day. *New York Times.* April 25, 2020. https://www.nytimes.com/2020/04/25/todayspaper/quotation-of-the-day-the-draft-filled-a-void-but-what-happens-next.html. Accessed May 27, 2023.

3. Frost R. The figure a poem makes. In: *The Collected Prose of Robert Frost.* Richardson M, ed. 2008; Cambridge, MA: Belknap Press.

4. McQuarrie C. *The Usual Suspects.* 1995; Gramercy Pictures.

5. Moore G. Cramming more components into integrated circuits. *Electronics* 1965; 38 (8).

6. Schilling D. How fast is data doubling. February 7, 2021. https://lodestar solutions.com/keeping-up-with-the-surge-of-information-and-human-knowledge/. Accessed May 23, 2023.

7. Yeats WB. *Essays and Introductions.* 1961; New York: Macmillan.

8. Sun Tzu. *The Art of War.* Sawyer RD, trans. 1994; New York: Basic Books.

9. Tyson M. ESPN interview prior to his fight with Evander Holyfield, 1996.

10. Williams RS, Willard HF, Snyderman R. Personalized health planning. *Science* 2003; 300: 549.

11. Snyderman R, Williams RS. *Prospective Medicine: The Next Healthcare Transformation. Academic Medicine* 2003; 78: 1079–1084.

12. Williams RS. Personal interview with the author, May 9, 2023.

CONCLUSION

1. Eiseley L. *The Star Thrower.* 1979; New York: Harvest Books.

ACKNOWLEDGMENTS

Say where Man's glory most begins and ends
And say my glory was I had such friends.

—WB YEATS

Having been privileged to have written over 25 books, I have learned that it is a deeply humbling experience and one that is never fully the work of the author alone. It takes the glory of having such friends, as Yeats said. This book has been deeply influenced by the many friends who have influenced and guided me through the years.

First, no one could ever hope for a better editor and friend than Lesley Iura at Berrett-Koehler, whose wisdom, humor, and kindness are unending. This book wouldn't have happened without her, from the moment I proposed it to its completion. This is my second book with Lesley, but I hope it is not the last.

Second, my developmental editor, Peter Economy, came extraordinarily highly recommended to me from Lesley and the other authors with whom he had previously worked. Peter exceeded all those recommendations with his incisive wisdom and surgical expertise with words. (And no, that name is not an allegory, although his economy with words is magical.)

About my wonderful and wonderfully talented chief of staff Linda Sokhor-Cooper, there are no words adequate to express how much easier she has made this process (and all others), but also how she had helped with the clarity and concision of the book. She is a uniquely multitalented person to whom Maureen and I will always be grateful. Shakespeare's words about Hermia in *A Midsummer Night's Dream* apply to her: "Though she be but little, she is fierce."

Many of the stories in the book derive from experiences with my friends and colleagues at the NFL Players Association (NFLPA) whose wisdom and generosity to me over the years is staggering. My debt to them is limitless and profound. Gene Upshaw, my best friend and then executive director of the NFLPA, commandeered me to become its first medical director on August 1, 2001, the day Korey Stringer, a tackle for the Vikings, died of heatstroke. The confidence and trust he showed in me to lead will never be forgotten, despite his untimely passing in 2008. I am grateful for his trust every day in my job.

DeMaurice "De" Smith succeeded Gene and kindly asked me to stay on in my role. The bond we formed through many battles to improve the health and safety of NFL players has been one of the highlights of my professional career. De is simply one of the most astute, intelligent, intuitive, and kind people I have ever met. He is not only a mentor but a trusted friend. He left the NFLPA and all the people in it better for being its leader for 14 years. I still depend on his wisdom.

Lloyd Howell is our current executive director and he has already shown himself to be a man with a rare ability to galvanize, synthesize, and integrate seemingly differing and even disparate ideas, concepts, and opinions into an actionable and meaningful whole. In a short period, he has earned massive and enduring respect from the NFLPA board and players and will be a great leader for many years into the future, using the lens of his business experience for the benefit of our players and their families.

A special thanks to Sean Sansiveri, general counsel and head of Business Affairs at the NFLPA, whose work in co-leading our health and safety efforts required courage, intelligence, creativity, tenacity, and humor, all of which he possesses to an uncommon degree. He is one of my closest friends, from whom I have learned immensely and continuously. He has made the work easier and infinitely more productive, while making my life better in the process. That's what a leader does . . .

Others at the NFLPA whom I admire immensely are Tom De-Paso, George Atallah, Dr. Don Davis, Mark Verstegen, Dr. Sid Hinds (our deputy medical director and chief health equity officer), Dr. Jeff Kutcher, Ernie Conwell, Tom Carter, Lester Archambeau, Andy Studebaker, Wesley Woodyard, Dwayne Allen, Brandon Chubb, Mark Cobb, Nolan Harrison, Kelly Mehrtens, Ned Ehrlich, Chris Fawal, Dr. Amber Cargill, and many others, each of whose wisdom is reflected in the book in various ways.

My profound thanks to the more than 10,000 players of the NFL whom it has been my honor and privilege to serve over 22 years, who have been the constant focus of my efforts. The six presidents under whom it has been my honor to serve are Trace Armstrong, Troy Vincent, Kevin Mawae, Domonique Foxworth, Eric Winston, and JC Tretter. They have been not only my bosses but my friends and mentors over the years, from whose wisdom and ferocious commitment to the players I have learned immensely. While mentioning all the players from whom I have learned would be impossible, several of the most influential are Drew Brees, Patrick Mahomes, Tom Brady, Aaron Rodgers, Jason McCourty, Devin McCourty, Matthew Slater, Michael Thomas, Richard Sherman, Mike Vrabel, Peyton Manning, Matt Hasselback, Gus Frerotte, and Jeff Saturday.

Dr. Geoff Ling is a founding member of the NFLPA's Mackey-White Health and Safety Committee and a legendary figure in military medicine. He is a sage and gimlet-eyed friend and mentor. When I ponder difficult issues in leading, I wait until I see what Geoff says so I know what I should think.

The NFLPA's funded research with the Football Players Health Study at Harvard has expanded the boundaries of our understanding of the effects of playing NFL football on our men's and their families' lives, and their work has changed the nature of our understanding of our motto of "Whole Player, Whole Family, Whole Life." Drs. Herman Taylor, Ross Zafonte, William Meehan, Rachel Grashow, and

Aaron Baggish (among many others) have showed courage and wisdom in taking on the tired assumptions and replacing them with facts. The players and I owe them a great debt.

My debt to my friends, colleagues, and mentors in emergency medicine, sports medicine, and the NFL are vast, but include Drs. Rob Strauss, Kirk Jensen, Jim Augustine, Jim Ellis, Jay Rao, John Brennan, Jim Bradley, Jim Muntz, Elliott Herschman, Elliot Pellman, Pat McKenzie, Andy Tucker, Bob Anderson, Neil Elattrache, Robin West, Allen Sills, and Paul Cusick, as well as athletic trainers Ronnie Barnes, Reggie Scott, Jim Whalen, Rick Burkholder, Kyle Johnston, Bryan Engel, Jim Maurer, Larry Ferazani, and Meghan Carroll.

Tom Peters is one of the legends of leading effectively and I am proud to call him a close friend. His insights are quoted many times in this book, but I only hope that I can someday live up to the many kind things he has said about me over the years. His character, humor, and contrarian views constantly inspire me and countless others. Tom also introduced me to Harry Rhoads, the cofounder of Washington Speakers Bureau, who taught me that the only reason to give a speech is to help someone. Harry was right, as always.

At Executive Speakers Bureau (executivespeakers.com/speaker/dr-thom-mayer), three people there have been ferocious about booking me to spread the message of this book. Genevieve Kurpuis, Angela Schelp, and Richard Schelp are the best friends and collaborators a speaker could possibly have.

In addition to my work with the NFLPA, I am very fortunate to work with my great friends and colleagues Drs. Eli Berg and Mike Granovsky, who have encouraged me in this work and who provide me a platform from which I can stress the lessons of leading in times of crisis. Their wisdom is exceeded only by their kindness and generosity.

Maureen and I work closely with Adam Sansiveri at Bernstein and Lindsay Owens Cressy at JP Morgan Private Bank, whose advice and counsel have been enriching.

Dr. Itzhak Shasha has been the closest of friends and the most incisive of mentors for more than 50 years and his advice, counsel, and encouragement have been invaluable. Whenever I have faced a difficult, seemingly complex decision, he has helped me see its true simplicity—and has kept me out of a lot of difficulties.

My work has played out on a highly public stage, requiring the scrutiny of the press. I have worked with many fine journalists in my career, including Chris Mortensen, Adam Schefter, Peter King, Andrea Kremer, Stepania Bell, Sally Jenkins, Pamela Brown, Jarrett Bell, Andrew Beaton, Stephen Dubner, Gina Kolata, and Mark Maske, all of whom treated me kindly and generously, even when I discussed controversial subjects.

High school and college friends and teammates from whom I continue to learn include Rod Freeman, Kevin Lane, Mike Woodruff, Mike Armstrong, Phil Bledsoe, Steve Voss, and Birt Hampton, Gary Erskine, Mike Paul, Jack Tharp, and Mark Levett. Professors from college and medical school whose impacts were profound and who are mentioned in the book are Drs. Enos Pray, Keith White, Joseph Campbell, David Sabiston, Madison Spach, Dale Johnson, Ralph Snyderman, and Sandy Williams. Thank you to all of them.

I learned an immense amount from my parents, Bette and James (Grandpa Jim) Mayer, both World War II veterans, as well as Maureen's parents, Georgette and Dr. John B. Henry, who gave me the greatest gift of my life—their daughter and my wife, Maureen.

Most important, always and forever, is my family whose love and advice has sustained me through the years. Their patience, kindness, and understanding with my long fascination—perhaps even preoccupation—with leading in times of crisis and their forgiveness for the long hours spent in lecturing, writing, and editing are deeply appreciated and treasured. Our sons, Josh, Kevin, and Greg, as well as Josh's wife Val and their children Eve, Audra, Clara, and Ryan, and Kevin's wife Nicola and their new son are the treasures of our lives and they were constantly upbeat and supportive throughout, offering important suggestions on improving the message.

Maureen, my beautiful, brilliant, and always inspiring wife is the source of all things good and great in my life. Whenever I was stuck on an issue, she always saw a way through and was ceaselessly positive about doing so. At every inflection point, her wisdom illuminated the pathway forward with clarity, concision, and humor. This book, like everything good in my life, would never have happened without her.

If I have failed to mention the many others whose influence was essential to this work, I apologize for the brevity. You know who you are and how much I appreciate you. Any insights arising from this book come from all these friends, colleagues, teachers, mentors, and teammates. Any failures are purely my own.

Thom Mayer, MD
Wilson, Wyoming
June 1, 2023

INDEX

ABOUT THE AUTHOR

Dr. Thom Mayer has been a leader in times of crisis for more than 25 years, navigating some of the most significant challenges imaginable. He is the medical director for the NFL Players Association, as well as an emergency physician-sports medicine leader of international renown. He served as the command physician at the Pentagon rescue and recovery operation on 9/11, incident commander  for the inhalational anthrax outbreak in Washington, DC, that same year, and led a Team Rubicon Mobile Emergency Team in Ukraine following the outbreak of war. He is among the most widely respected leaders in times of crisis and is a highly sought after speaker and consultant across many businesses and industries.

Dr. Mayer was the originator of the entire NFL Concussion Guidelines program, and thus has changed the nature of the management of concussions worldwide. He also devised the emergency action plan program for the NFL, which recently resulted in a player's life being saved following cardiac arrest on an NFL field. During the COVID-19 outbreak, he and his team developed testing and treatment guidelines that resulted in two successful and highly entertaining NFL seasons, while keeping the players and their families safe.

He was recently nominated to the Pro Football Hall of Fame in Canton, Ohio, and is a member of the Indiana Football Hall of Fame and the Hanover College Athletic Hall of Fame. *USA Today* named him one of the "100 Most Important People in the NFL." Tom Peters, the internationally acclaimed expert on leading, referred to his work as "gaspworthy."

Dr. Mayer has served on three Department of Defense Science Board Task Forces on Bioterrorism, Homeland Security, and Consequences of Weapons of Mass Destruction.

He has written 25 books, two of which won the American College of Healthcare Executives' prestigious James Hamilton Award for the best leadership book of the year, including *Battling Healthcare Burnout: Learning to Love the Job You Have While Creating the Job You Love,* also published by Berrett-Koehler. His work has been featured on CNN, ESPN, and Fox News, and in the *Wall Street Journal*, *New York Times*, and *Washington Post*, as well as in every major academic publication worldwide.

Despite these many accomplishments, he continues to push the envelope of innovation in leading in times of crisis in all walks of life.

He is a graduate of Hanover College and the Duke University School of Medicine and a Professor of Emergency Medicine at George Washington University School of Medicine and a Senior Lecturing Fellow at Duke University.

He and his wife Maureen live in Wilson, Wyoming, and Great Falls, Virginia.

Berrett–Koehler
Publishers

Berrett-Koehler is an independent publisher dedicated to an ambitious mission: *Connecting people and ideas to create a world that works for all.*

Our publications span many formats, including print, digital, audio, and video. We also offer online resources, training, and gatherings. And we will continue expanding our products and services to advance our mission.

We believe that the solutions to the world's problems will come from all of us, working at all levels: in our society, in our organizations, and in our own lives. Our publications and resources offer pathways to creating a more just, equitable, and sustainable society. They help people make their organizations more humane, democratic, diverse, and effective (and we don't think there's any contradiction there). And they guide people in creating positive change in their own lives and aligning their personal practices with their aspirations for a better world.

And we strive to practice what we preach through what we call "The BK Way." At the core of this approach is *stewardship,* a deep sense of responsibility to administer the company for the benefit of all of our stakeholder groups, including authors, customers, employees, investors, service providers, sales partners, and the communities and environment around us. Everything we do is built around stewardship and our other core values of *quality, partnership, inclusion,* and *sustainability.*

This is why Berrett-Koehler is the first book publishing company to be both a B Corporation (a rigorous certification) and a benefit corporation (a for-profit legal status), which together require us to adhere to the highest standards for corporate, social, and environmental performance. And it is why we have instituted many pioneering practices (which you can learn about at www.bkconnection.com), including the Berrett-Koehler Constitution, the Bill of Rights and Responsibilities for BK Authors, and our unique Author Days.

We are grateful to our readers, authors, and other friends who are supporting our mission. We ask you to share with us examples of how BK publications and resources are making a difference in your lives, organizations, and communities at www.bkconnection.com/impact.

Dear reader,

Thank you for picking up this book and welcome to the worldwide BK community! You're joining a special group of people who have come together to create positive change in their lives, organizations, and communities.

What's BK all about?

Our mission is to connect people and ideas to create a world that works for all.

Why? Our communities, organizations, and lives get bogged down by old paradigms of self-interest, exclusion, hierarchy, and privilege. But we believe that can change. That's why we seek the leading experts on these challenges—and share their actionable ideas with you.

A welcome gift

To help you get started, we'd like to offer you a **free copy** of one of our bestselling ebooks:

www.bkconnection.com/welcome

When you claim your **free ebook**, you'll also be subscribed to our blog.

Our freshest insights

Access the best new tools and ideas for leaders at all levels on our blog at ideas.bkconnection.com.

Sincerely,

Your friends at Berrett-Koehler

Certified

Corporation